SHE'S
A KEEPER

~ confessions from a
Southern Girl's Closet

To: Julia-
Good luck to
you.
Lee st john
12/6/15

by Lee St. John

published by
Shady Grove Press

Visit Lee's website at *www.LeeStJohnauthor.com*
to sign up for her email list
and get a FREE gift from her and to get a heads-up email when
Lee St. John releases a new book.

This book is a book of non-fiction.
Names, characters, places, and incidents are the
recollections of the author and are recounted as told in vignettes
and shared by permission
of the participants. Certain details may be altered in the instances
of those who wish to remain anonymous.

SHE'S A KEEPER
~ confessions from a Southern Girl's Closet

Published by Shady Grove Press

www.LeeStJohnauthor.com

ISBN-13:   978-0692549018   (Shady Grove Press)
ISBN-10:   0692549013

To:

All my boys, including Boo, the cat, and Jager, the grand dog.

Notably to:

*My sweetie Wheatie, Kelly, who left me with all this testosterone.
I miss you terribly.*

Lee St. John

TABLE OF CONTENTS

TABLE OF CONTENTS (cont.)

Before You Read Any Further!

As an only child, Lee St. John has always been used to getting her own way. And it didn't help that she was born to 40 year old parents. Growing up, she wore them out as she consistently spoke her mind without a "pause" button and horrified them with her outrageous behavior. Now as an adult, nothing has changed. But maybe she is getting her comeuppance. The behavior she exhibited upset her parents. Now she is the one upset by her children because they are not giving her the time of day. Over the years as the only female in her family, she kept mementos of her parents, her family, her friends, and her students in various places around her home – her closet, her attic, her basement, her garage, and - even at one time – her classroom. Each of these keepsakes trigger a delicious story that she wants to share with her two boys and YOU.

Each story is grouped together by theme. The title tells the tale and the discovery is a reminder of the cherished event. Hopefully, NOW she has her boys' attention!

Lee St. John

CLOSET:

The Joke's On You

"You Better Watch Out, You Better Not Cry..."

1990 – L.L. Bean Boots

When my oldest was five years old (THE HEIR), I decided to make his Christmas really special. You know how we, as mothers, made home-made cookies and left them on a Christmas designed plate with a glass of milk and maybe a carrot for Rudolf? Well, been there, done that. This year was different.

When we tucked him in and he fell asleep, I pulled out from the closet my husband's L.L. Bean boots and the largest size baking soda box that the grocery stores carried. I laid down a boot on the rug, poured baking soda around the perimeter, lifted the boot, placed the matching boot a step ahead, and again poured the baking soda. After several times, it looked as if Santa had sloughed off snow on his way from our fireplace to the Christmas tree and laid out his presents.

The fireplace stood empty because we didn't use it. We had a red enamel wood burning stove. When the logs were burning, the stove lit up a beautiful Christmas red and then became a part of the room's holiday décor.

Christmas morning came and THE HEIR jumped out of bed, ran into the living room, and saw all the presents and Santa's footsteps! Overjoyed, his eyes widened! Santa came! He looked so cute in his Stewart plaid red pajamas with red piping on the collar and long sleeves and also wearing his solid navy blue housecoat. He wore no house shoes, just those sweet bare feet which ran down the hall.

Our usual festivities of opening all the presents ensued and then friends and family popped over to see what THE HEIR received. He bragged about Santa's footsteps on the rug. And as the days wore on and more people dropped by, Santa's footprints were still on the rug. He continued to show them off.

Nailed it.

When THE SPARE (our second son) turned five, I remembered how THE HEIR received such joy from my creativity that I tried to pull this same trick.

We did the same thing again. But our savvy THE SPARE in his cotton long-sleeved blue dinosaur pajamas, just looked at the situation and the first thing out of his mouth was, "Why hasn't it melted?"

Didn't think he'd catch that.

Center of Attention

1930's University of Georgia Teaching Certificate

My mother taught school for 37 years before retiring in 1972. She loved being a school teacher. She was 30 years old before she married. Born in 1913, she was one of a few women in her generation who even attended college. More remarkably, she also obtained her Master's in education. She attended Emory University and the University of Georgia to get that piece of parchment, which was kept with her other important papers in my closet.

In those very early days of teaching, one just obtained a teaching certificate and taught any grade. When she first started, she taught elementary school students. She then went on to teach American Government in high school, a required course for graduation that was taught in 12th grade.

Her entire career was spent in one Georgia county. She began her teaching career in 1935. One funny story happened early in her high school career. If you know your Georgia history, school used to only be in session eight months of the year - not nine. It was based around the agricultural summer season where most children were needed at home on their parents' farms. My county, twenty-five-plus miles outside of Atlanta, was very rural. One day in the middle of a classroom activity, one of her high school students jumped two stories from her open window and left. He went home to work. I guess he figured the farm was more appealing than sitting in a non- air conditioned classroom learning government. I bet that Georgia boy got a red-neck working outside.

My mother was adored by her students. She taught for so long and with such loving enthusiasm and devotion to her classes, that her students started calling her "Mother" because she did mother as many as she could. They even inserted her name in the school fight song, which they kept singing even after she retired.

Some members of the Senior Class of 1969, out of loving respect, decided to play a little hoax. Mother used those geography maps that scrolled up and down. She used them almost daily in her American and world government discussions. This class had some pranksters who thought it would be funny to pull one over her. While she was on hall duty, a couple of boys from 5th period taped a Playboy Centerfold onto one of those world maps and then rolled it back up into its cover. They planned to ask a question in class that involved having her pull down THAT PARTICULAR MAP to answer the question they posed.

What they hadn't counted on was 3rd period. Someone in 3rd period innocently asked a question that caused my mother to pull down the map with the nude model plastered in the middle of a world map. Since she stood in front of the map and no one expected the ruse, the students didn't see it and she tore the picture off without the rest of 3rd period knowing the difference.

So, there was no way that the prank had spread around the school. Fourth period passed. But then, 5th period showed up and those funny guys, who just KNEW they were going to pull-one-over on my mother, asked some question that was supposed to bring down the "Playboy" map. Of course it actually backfired on them, because without a doubt, they were the perpetrators that placed the centerfold there in the first place.

Because it wasn't meant maliciously, I don't think those that were caught got into too much trouble. Really.

"He who laughs last, laughs best."

1983 - Embroidered Fish Lure silk necktie

While working at the Atlanta Apparel Mart, my showroom secretary job turned into a full-fledged sales representative job for a nationally known company that manufactured menswear. I had some major accounts whose stores were in Atlanta, Pensacola, Florida, and Jacksonville, Florida but I also traveled to some Mom & Pop stores in-between.

I was married and we lived outside the Atlanta perimeter in Cobb County. My husband had bought his first house there as a bachelor. His new house did not have a garage. Instead, it had a carport. I had various cars that we bought for my long hauls on the road around both states. I drove a blue 1978 Chevrolet Malibu Classic Station Wagon. I carried my sample merchandise in suitcases, which I kept in my car, so I did not have to lug them in and out each day. Sometimes I had lots of samples. They were either men's neckwear or casual shorts, slacks, cotton shirts, or knit shirts from the sportswear line.

The majority of my business was selling men's neckwear. I was involved in so much neckwear, that my lucky husband was able to get samples from me or certainly buy some at cost that he liked better. We loaded him up with neckwear. He was a "Fancy Dan."

The high-end neckwear that I sold was designed by Oscar de la Renta. My favorite neck tie that my husband selected, was a navy blue 100% silk woven tie with fish lures embroidered on it. He had several others I liked, but that was a good looking tie hanging in the closet (and on him!).

Most of my samples, though, were on the low-end of the price spectrum. They were made from polyester and you bought them as a clip-on. My company was the first to make damn-ugly-clip-on ties for the man who never learned how to tie one on. I had dozens of samples of that kind in the suitcases in my car.

I thought we were in a safe neighborhood. I never locked my car doors and I didn't lock my car door the night before my next day in town sales trip. Getting in my car the next morning, I realized my suitcases were stolen.

Thankfully, those sample ties were replaced by my company. But what I realized that couldn't be replaced and wished I had seen was the look on those thieves faces when they realized all they had stolen were neckties! I doubt the kind of thieves that would steal from a car in a carport would even WEAR a tie, especially a clip-on one.

JIVE Talking

1993 Scrabble Board Game

It was 1993. Scrabble Night. Another couple and hubby and I played Scrabble in their home. We brought over our board game from home, now kept in our lake house closet. It was late and we were almost done. With only four letters left, I played on a triple word score square the word JIVE. I also used all of my letters and that gave me extra points. My husband and I seemingly won the game with that last move.

But our male host was going to have none of it. He said, "There is no such word as 'jive.'" His wife begged to differ. She agreed with us that there was such a word. But he was going to have none of it and called it an evening. She was upset with her husband's actions, but we knew him for a long time and he thought he was always right. We just sorta indulged him, but the evening was over. It hadn't come to a natural conclusion, but an abrupt one with his guests beating him in Scrabble in his own home. He didn't like that one bit.

We left. Because I saw behavior like this before from him, I decided I'd try to goad him a little more. I was a practical jokester. I looked over the rules on the way home while hubby drove and the rules said that if the word could be found in the dictionary, it was a word. This was way before iPhones, so I would have called him then and there and told him I was sure the word was in my dictionary.
I did find the word in my dictionary when we got home and even

though it was very late, I called the host and told him there was the word 'jive' in my dictionary. Within a few minutes, he called back and read the rule that said, "If a word cannot be found in the HOST's dictionary, it is not a word.' He said he could not find the word in his dictionary.

Good Grief! How much longer was this going to go on? I think he was serious. And he was a very smart man and won a lot of arguments, but I wasn't about to take this one lying down. I hatched a plan.

This Scrabble-playing couple was in our dinner club of five couples. It was time for another dinner club. Ironically, it was held at the home of the same couple where we played Scrabble. Not that it mattered where the dinner club was, but it seemed poetic justice in some ways after I put my plan to work.

I called the other three couples, not the host couple – it was a surprise– and BEGGED them to PLEASE incorporate the word 'jive' into their conversations throughout the night... for instance, "We went to see a 'jive' of a movie last week", etc. One of our couple friends was our church's associate pastor and I asked him, while he gave the blessing before our food, to say something like, "Bless this 'jiving' food, etc."

He did.

All the couples played along. It was so funny to see the look on the host's face when 'jive' came out of their mouths in normal conversation. When it happened so much, he realized he had been taken.

He looked at me and said, "You win."

(Happy Dance!)

P.S. I really don't see how some people can be so stubborn!

Family Tree

2006 Tombstones

My husband's family had deep roots. They said they could trace their lineage all the way back to Charlemagne, who died in 814 A.D. I knew one thing, they kept naming new family members with the same old family names.

My in-laws named my husband Hugh Lee, a very Southern double name. ALL his family and Kappa Alpha fraternity brothers at Auburn called him the double name. Hugh Lee this and Hugh Lee that. His father even called home one day from work, in the 1959, to ask about him. Speaking with his wife he asked her, "How is Hugh Lee doing today? What's Hugh Lee up to?"

A co-worker at the next desk overheard his conversation and when my future father-in-law put the receiver back on the cradle, the other man said, "That sure was nice of you to adopt that refugee." I guess Hugh Lee sounded a lot like Hu Le.

At another dinner club, this time in 2007, we had several couples over for a Halloween-themed dinner because I asked to have it close to Halloween Night. I always LOVED Halloween. I decorated my whole house with pumpkins, witches' hats, and skeletons. I even hung Halloween plates on the wall racks in my kitchen. I stored them in my kitchen cabinet to be used each year.

I created a great homemade graveyard with sayings from a book with real but funny epitaphs in it. Some of the epitaphs that I wrote on my tombstones said, "Here Lies Jake. He forgot to put on the brake." Another one said, "Here lies the body of our Anna. Done to death by a banana. It wasn't the fruit that laid her low, but the skin of the thing that made her go." But my all time favorite epitaph said, "I told you I was sick."

I kept them downstairs in a storage closet until the fifth year of decorating the graveyard when someone stole them. I was done.

Our new neighborhood had a small real graveyard in one area. It only had five graves. But I used this as the entertainment for my dinner guests. I made sure every couple brought a flashlight and their golf cart. After cocktails and before dinner, we drove over to the site where the five graves were. We pulled out our flashlights as we climbed the hill, and I told a fake story about the history of the markers. I blabbed something about there was a fire and all five members of the household died. There were no names on the markers and there were only the death dates, which were sometime around the late 1800's, so it was easy enough to make up names from that time period to relate who might be buried there. It seemed believable. And they never questioned it.

When we arrived back to our house for dinner, I told them the truth about the fake story and that I knew nothing about who was lying in the graves. They were amused and we continued to enjoy the evening.

The couples had not been to our home before and in the living room we had several oil portraits. Two of them were our children, but one was an ancestor of my husband's. Except for the beard, this portrait looked like Abraham Lincoln in his dark suit, a cream colored shirt with pearl buttons, and a grey ascot-type necktie. Our guy in the painting just had a Chin Strap beard. This style derived its name from the chin strap that comes with a helmet. The sideburns of the ancestor in our oil portrait went all the way round and connected at the chin to form a continuous line of hair.

One of our guests asked about this portrait. I explained that this gentleman was my husband's great-great-grandfather, who was the last surviving doctor during the Yellow Fever epidemic in Shreveport, Louisiana. He was holding in his hand, the Southern Medical Journal.

Our guest then said, "After tonight, how do I know I can believe you?"

Touche´.

The Royal Wedding

1986 "Majesty" Magazine

I was the most devoted Anglophile of my immediate friends. No one – I mean – NO ONE kept up with the English Royal Family as much as I did. I have always been interested in the Tudors and English Renaissance and I loved reading about the family trees of the English monarchs.

I had subscribed to "Majesty" Magazine since 1981. Mother and I shared this beautifully photographed magazine about the European royals with more emphasis on the British. The cost was high, but with two sharing, we managed to feel like we got our money's worth. I kept all the back copies in my storage room. Magazine after magazine of Princess Diana on most of the covers, occasionally another royal family member, but she was the one whose photograph sold magazines. This magazine had the nod of approval from the British family so it was full of great interviews, historical information, and current stories... better than "People" magazine and their covering of the royal families.

When mother was due to give birth to me, Queen Elizabeth II's coronation was to be televised, the first ever and it was also the world's first major international event to be broadcast on television. She need not have worried. She was able to see it. I came along 5 days later.

I was so devoted, I awoke in the early morning of July 29, 1981 to see Prince Charles marry the Lady Diana Spencer. Mother and I were in London when Prince William was born on June 21, 1982. There were celebrations during the time we visited there and that was exciting.

As one memento of our London vacation, I bought a Wedgwood Blue Jasperware Trinket Box depicting a Horse Drawn Chariot which was encircled by a simple single Laurel wreath. It had an incised mark stating 'Wedgwood made in England'. I placed it in my guest room. It housed my guests' jewelry or coins when they visited.

When William's wedding to Catherine Middleton on April 29, 2011 at Westminster Abbey was a topic many were interested in, I decided to have a little fun with this. A month before the wedding, I wrote on my Facebook page that I was "invited to the ceremony. My invitation AND ticket to enter the cathedral came in the mail today." I wrote this because at the time, the Windors were not only inviting other royals, but also they had announced they were sending invitations to a few commoners. I had been in Westminster Abbey while touring London in 1981 and I saw the alcoves in the cathedral. I kept elaborating that "my printed ticket said that I would be sitting in alcove 'E' and my seat number was 37." I remarked that I was "totally surprised to be one of the 'regular/commoner' guests who applied to be invited to the wedding."

Even if my friends knew how gaga I was over the royals, most knew this was a hoax. But I was able to fool one Facebook friend. She was so excited for me and wrote profusely to me on Facebook about my getting every detail of the wedding so that I could tell her about it when I came home.

I should feel bad. But I don't.

Hide and Seek

1984 Auburn Shakers

Auburn/Georgia game. It was called this if you were an Auburn fan. It was called Georgia/Auburn if you were a Georgia fan.

My ALMOST-BIG-SISTER and her husband were rabid Georgia fans. Like so many, they bled red and black. Their ritual was to leave for each game day at the same time, park in the same place every time, tailgate with the same couples each time, and always bring the same tailgate food. And sometimes, just sometimes, they allowed their Auburn friends to join them, but only if it looked like beating Auburn was a sure thing. Even then, it stayed uncomfortable until the scoreboard blazed a Georgia win at the end of the struggle. We invited them to our Auburn tailgate group every year, but they never made it...they had their own plans for away games, too. Superstitious? Too much blue and orange? Who knew? Since she was my ALMOST-BIG-SISTER, Auburn HUBBY and I were invited to their pre-game tailgate but only on occasion (a sure UGA win, remember?).

We enjoyed visiting with them and some old hometown folks before the game, but if Auburn won, they were nowhere to be found post-game at their pre-game parking spot. Gone! If the Bulldogs won, we were certainly welcomed back to polish off some more potato salad and hear all their barking.

I became an Auburn fan when I married. I went to the University of Georgia grad school and was a big fan until…I was condemned once at an Auburn/Georgia game in Athens. I wore the Georgia regalia even with my new Auburn friends. I was still on the Bulldog side until I was bullied by some Georgia fans because I associated with these Auburn people. It was ugly and I didn't get over it. I became a good Auburn wife after that especially when my HUBBY paid for all my charges on the Master or Visa credit cards each month. I also had my colors done by a beauty technician at Nordstrom's in Atlanta who told me that ORANGE was my color! That did it!

One of those years, HUBBY and I planned to head to Athens for the game. We had the tickets – very hard to come by – but for some reason – oh, I remembered what it was: we thought Auburn might lose badly in Athens – we weren't able to attend. It was a night game and those very cold night games were just no fun driving 2 hours home after a loss. So, we decided to watch it on TV. (We lost.)

But my ALMOST-BIG-SISTER, who invited us to the pre-game tailgate, didn't know that we changed our minds. It was a last minute/last day decision. I kept her in the dark about our plans. She expected us to still rendezvous with her Georgia crew and a few hours before kick-off when she expected us, I texted her.

ME: Where did you park?
ABS: Where are YOU?
ME: It matters more that we know where YOU are.
ABS: We are yada, yada, yada (she gives directions)
ME: Oh, we are pretty close. Will text again when we get closer.

I waited 30 minutes. At home. On the sofa.

ME: WHERE are you? (she again gave directions)

ME: Oh, I see you. (The tailgate was in the afternoon of the night game.) Do you see us?
ABS: No, I don't. Where are you?

If we had been there, HUBBY and I would totally be decked out in orange and blue. I would have carried our good luck shakers that were kept in the foyer closet for each game. We would have also carried our Auburn stadium seats. I mean, we'd have screamed Auburn.

ME: We are coming down the hill. I am also carrying my pimento cheese sandwiches in a Tupperware container. I am afraid I might drop them.
ABS: Where are you I don't see you.
ME: You should be able to see us. Can't you spot us? I am the one wearing orange and blue (ha, ha – get it?). We are closer. I am waving at you. I see you. Wait a minute….hold on.
(click)

I waited at least 15 minutes before texting her again.

ME: Some Bulldog fan is getting into it with HUBBY.
(silence)

ME: You won't believe this, I spilled the sandwiches. Some Georgia fans are eating the ones that spilled on the sidewalk. Where are you? I can't see you now. Do you see us…uh, oh, here comes that guy again. He won't go away! He's shaking his fist at HUBBY. No, wait, he just wants our sandwiches. He's picking them up from the sidewalk. Gross! (click)

Now it was very close to game time when I called again.

ME: I bet you aren't going to wait for us.
ABS: What happened to you? We are going on into the game. We have to get to our seats to see the band. We have a routine.

ME: What about all these sandwiches that I brought? Who is going to eat them now? I picked up most of the ones that spilled and that the Georgia fans didn't eat. There aren't many left but the ones that are, I wiped them off.

ABS: We are heading over to the stadium and almost inside. We have to go in and get our seats. We have a routine.

ME: Well, thanks a lot for waiting. We are here now and you are not. I don't know what I am going to do with all these sandwiches.

We didn't communicate for the rest of the night because we were both busy watching the game. The next day I told her the truth. I wondered why she doesn't trust anything I say any more.

CLOSET:

Oral Gratification

What goes up must come…

1963 "Highlights" Magazine

I froze whenever I visited the dentist as a young girl. Dentists were different back then. First of all, they worked on Saturdays. People mostly worked Monday – Friday in the 50's and 60's. All the stores were closed on Sundays. Since my mother was a teacher and worked during the week, we went to the dentist on Saturdays, except in the summer.

My dentist was exceptionally scary. He had a thick head of dark hair, with dark bushy eyebrows, and dark brown eyes. I think he even scared his hygienist. She never smiled. She looked so worried after the cleaning as if he chewed her out all the time checking over her preparation.

Years later, I found that there was more than one way to clean one's teeth. My PARTNER-IN-CRIME-IN-ATLANTA, when I was a young woman and first moved there after college, introduced me to her dentist. I found it more enjoyable because of the soft music, gentle flossing, and reclining chair. Wow! Nothing to make me feel nervously sick!

To make up for my childhood anxiety, mother tried her best to calm my fears of going to the dentist. For my cooperation, she treated me to something special so that I did not pitch a fit about going to the dental appointment.

One particular Saturday, she told me we would go out to lunch before our cleaning. Now, there wasn't much in the way of eating out in our little county, so we stopped for a BBQ sandwich and Brunswick stew at a local joint.

However, no matter how much I enjoyed the meal to get my mind off what was coming, it still wasn't enough to put me at ease. We arrived and I went first to get it over with. After my appointment and waiting on her, my gums swelled and ached from the flossing routine. They bled for a while. But, on a lighter note, I did enjoy reading HIGHLIGHTS while I waited. I enjoyed the "Goofus and Gallant" section. I liked trying to find the hidden pictures in the magazine when somebody else hadn't already circled them. Bummer. I subscribed to the magazine which was mailed to my home but the dentist seemed to always have the latest edition. I kept those magazines for a long time in a box in the hall closet, at first to reread them, and secondly, after keeping them for so long, thinking my future children might like them - circled hidden pictures or not.

In the 1960's, we dressed up everywhere when we went out in public. I wore one of my best outfits. I had on a pleated MacAulay Hunting Tartan plaid skirt with a navy vest. Under it I wore a white ¾ length sleeve 100% cotton shirt which had ruffles covering the buttons down the front. I had white socks up to my calves with black Mary Jane leather shoes.

When I was in the chair for the cleaning, the hygienist was as sweet as she could be. But the cloud hung over both of us. Personally, I didn't see how she worked for that man. When the dentist came in to examine her work and my teeth, there was a knot in my stomach. His rhetoric always was, "Breathe through your nose! BREATHE THROUGH YOUR NOSE!" He was loud and boisterous and scared the bejesus out of me every time. Mother said he was unhappy because he always had an upset stomach. His lower torso was near your ear in the dentist chair so you heard the grumbling of something going on in his intestines. He yelled at me all the time so I felt no sorrow for him. He was irate and I was just as upset.

Then my nerves got the best of me, my stomach started to knot. Then I felt nauseous. Then, I WAS nauseous…all over him and ME! The Brunswick stew that I ate came back up in my projectile vomiting. Ironically, it looked the same coming out as it went in….shredded pork, bits of corn, etc.

There I was in this great outfit and there was Brunswick Stew all over me, too! And having a tomato base from the stew, we never did get that stain out of that white shirt.

I did not worry about my dentist. He got what he deserved.

Playing Dentist

1967 Varsity Letter

With the earlier bad experiences I had in the dental department, I decided to take matters into my own hands.

In 1967 I was a Freshman in high school and I was taking first year French along with just about every other 9th grader who was on the college prep track. I had made Varsity cheerleader for that school year. I wore my uniform every Friday before a weekend football or basketball game. This uniform was a black wool skirt that was knee-length (why is it the cheerleaders wore long skirts in the 60's and the guys wore SHORT –and TIGHT- athletic shorts in basketball?). It had a black fitted wool vest and our large red high school letter on the front. We all wore white Oxford cloth long-sleeve shirts with a round collar. Our school initials were embroidered in red on one of our cuffs. We wore white knee socks with our black and white clod-hoppers (or Saddle Shoes) with red and black plaid shoe strings. Oh, I don't want to forget the red cover-up pants over our panties. I kept my letter when I returned my uniform after graduation.

High school classes were designed in 1967 to have 7 periods for 1 hour each. All classes, including French I, lasted the whole year. We sat in rows of desks about 10 seats deep X's 4 rows. There were a lot of Freshmen.

The FUTURE-VALEDICTORIAN of my Senior class of 1971 sat behind me. He was an excellent student and later became a doctor.

Just about every Freshman had something I wanted badly to fit in: glasses and braces. I didn't have the need to wear them but wanted them just the same to be like everyone else.

I had such straight teeth, dentists in my future told me, "You are NOT helping me pay for my dental practice." I did not have many dental problems and only 6 fillings my entire life. But there was one boy in my school who I dated that didn't have ANY fillings. I was impressed with that.

I did have one problem from birth. I inherited my mother's muscle frenum. This was the space between your front teeth caused by the muscle behind them. Mine was on the upper front two teeth. It was so wide that I stuck my tongue in sideways.

I wanted to do something about it. FUTURE-VALEDICTORIAN, my back seat neighbor, wore braces. The braces in the 1960's came with a string of tiny rubber bands which when placed on the upper and lower metal braces, would pull teeth together, I supposed. Remember, I never wore braces. But I did want to get rid of that gap. I thought I looked like the Mad Magazine cover boy, Alfred E. Newman.

I asked FUTURE-VALEDICTORIAN, "May I borrow some of your rubber bands?" (Why did I ask to borrow? I was not going to give them back.) I placed two bands around my front 4 teeth during that one hour in French class, for two weeks, and my gap closed.

And the best part was the space NEVER opened up again. I saved my parents hundreds of dollars and that was when I thought about going into dental school in college.

That thought didn't last long after my next report card.

Clean-up in Boys' Bathroom
1967 Home Hair Dryer with Connecting Bonnet

Sitting by the pool at my apartment complex one summer weekend in 1982 in my 2-piece blue bathing suit with white butterflies on it and pullover top, which had a drawstring in the neckline casing, two friends and I were sunning. The bra part of my suit had a self fabric bow. My bikini bottoms had a side zipper and came up to just under my belly button. We slathered on Tropicana Lotion/Oil to get as dark a tan as we could. No sunscreen for us as we didn't know any better.

Another crazy thing I did two decades before was I washed my hair in Tide detergent to bleach it lighter while lying in the sun. After washing the Tide out of my hair, I rolled it with cleaned-out large frozen orange juice cans to make my hair straighter. I dried my hair with a home dryer that puffed air through a tube that connected to a bonnet. Mine was pink and only about 300- 400 watts. My hair was so thick that it took at least an hour, or maybe two, before the hair dried and could be brushed out. This meant if you were having a Saturday night date, you spent your Saturday afternoon under the dryer. That pink dryer took up a lot of room in my closet for years.

While sunning, one gal told me this story about her first year teaching. As an elementary school teacher she was responsible for a first grade classroom in the 1970's. She prepared an assignment for the entire class to take at one time. However, there was a problem. One of the boys in her class was still in the boys' restroom in the back of the room.

She waited a moment for his return before passing out the papers. While waiting, another little boy asked if he could use the restroom. With the one in the classroom occupied, the other young man had to go down the hall to the closest one near his class.

The first boy came out of the restroom and took his seat. Now the second was absent and while waiting a good while longer, it did not seem like he was going to return anytime soon. Where could he be? She needed to start the assignment.

In the 1970's there were no teacher assistants. My teacher friend asked her neighboring classroom teacher to look in on her students while she went to find the boy.

She wandered down the hall heading toward the boys' restroom when she heard whimpering. What she was about to do would almost be unheard of today. She ducked her head in to see if this was her student. It was and she found him crying.

He was in the stall and the door was closed. She asked him gently why he was crying and he answered that while zipping his pants up…yep, you guessed it, he had zipped himself. OUCH!

She coaxed him out of the stall and then as a concerned educator/mother/nurse, she asked to see his wound. Seeing that it was bleeding, she told him to stay still and she ran to the school office in search of some medicine to put on the wound.

The medicine of choice in the 1970's was not Neosporin or something similar, but a red, stingy, burn-to-the-touch item called Mercurochrome. There were no school nurses, so she had to take the medicine back to the boy with cotton balls to administer it.

The boy was small so my teacher friend had to get on her knees to see the scratch and applied the Mercurochrome. It stung! It burned! It was worth crying over! It left a red dye on the surface of the wound. She applied it the best she could and like many of our mothers did, because of the stinging sensation, she blew cool air on it to make it feel better immediately.

She administered disinfectant, puffed, and blew on the wound several times when a male janitor walked in to clean the restroom and saw my friend down on both knees, the back of her head bobbed up and down from puffing and blowing and then he yelled out, "B— J! B— J—!"

Do Not Try This At Home

1980 Add-A-Bead Necklace

After my dentist scares, I took some dental matters into my own hands. It depended on the audience when I'd tell this story. If the crowd was under 21, I told it one way, and for the over 21, another.

It involved alcohol.

Once, when I was still single, my PARTNER-IN-CRIME and I, were out and about frequenting the night life. We visited several popular beer dives in Buckhead, a high-end shopping and residential district in Atlanta. At one of these, there was a situation that I did not use my best judgment.

It happened on a Thursday night and I remembered thinking, "This is my last Coca-Cola (under 21)/beer (over 21)" for the evening. As I held my coke bottle/beer bottle in my right hand and started to lift it up to take a swig, someone walked behind me, hit my right elbow, pushed my arm up fast, and with that movement, the long-neck bottle hit my front right tooth and made a chip.

I didn't know it at that moment because I spilled beer all over my Kelly-green wrap around cotton skirt with navy blue piping on the hem and on the tie at the waist. The skirt was monogrammed in my initials near the hem and that's where the beer mostly landed. I wore a 100% cotton long-sleeved button down Polo shirt, which had the little polo guy on the left breast. It, too, had beer stains. I was tan and didn't need hose.

I loved my Kelly-green Pappagallo shoes with a gold buckles on the bridge of the shoes. On my right hand ring finger, I wore a 14 carat gold 1 carat oval diamond ring bought from Maier and Berkele given to me by my parents on my most recent birthday. My other favorite piece of jewelry was a 14 carat gold and amethyst add-a-bead necklace, which has been kept in my closet jewelry box. I pulled back my shoulder length hair with a gold hair band (which I kept, too). I have still worn them both on occasion.

I looked down at the beer on my shirt and skirt and then ran my tongue along the bottom of that front right tooth and felt a concave shape in my normally straight-edged tooth. Oh, what did it look like? How big was it? I had to get home!

My home was a 1940's brick apartment building with 12 units. It was old and did not have central air conditioning…only window units and it also had steam heat. The walls were made of plaster and ceilings were 12 feet high. Woods floors throughout, but no dishwasher. My bathroom was old, too. In my dimly lit bathroom, I saw the problem. I was in trouble. There was a half-moon shape gap at the bottom edge of my tooth. Not terribly big, but noticeable. I decided to take matters in my own hands.

I pulled out my angel nail file and started filing down that tooth. I was already anesthetized (over 21 story addition), so I wasn't worried about pain – yet – until I realized I better stop. But I did do enough filing to whittle away the gap and make it look straight again, even if my right tooth was a little shorter than my left.

I thought of it this way: not only did I save myself a lot of money but also, in my inebriated state, I thought again that I would have made a fine dentist.

Calling Roll

1994 Dog Pillows

No matter how one wished for the first few days of school to run smoothly, there were blips. There were so many names to learn when you are teaching older students, because of all the class changes.

While teaching Gifted in middle school, we serviced the Gifted identified child for 4 ½ hours a week requested by the government. Now, there were several ways to accommodate them: they were pulled out of their regular classrooms for part of the time every day for 5 days, or pulled out for longer periods of time for less days, or all day for one day a week. We chose the latter. That meant the first day of class happened in week one. The second day of class happened in week two.

When I taught high school we either saw them every day (non-block schedule) or every other day (block schedule). Even then it took me a while to realize that I thought I saw this one student more often than the others; but soon realized he was a twin and I had both boys on roll but in different classes.

My classroom had the desks with chairs that slid underneath but I also had a large four-pillowed sea blue sofa with cream ticking in the material. I no longer used the sofa at my home but I brought it back anyway and placed it in my basement when that year was over. The pillows were still in good condition and large enough for our Soft

Coated Wheaten Terrier, Kelly, to sleep on as a dog pillow. When she dirtied it, there were three more from my hall closet to replace it.

Several of my students rushed to class so they could claim a seat on the sofa. It got them to class on time even if they fought over who was going to sit on the sofa that day. We had smaller classes in the Gifted program on a daily basis, but it was still sometimes difficult at first to remember a student's name when you would see them one week and not see them again for another week.

As always, I took roll the first week in middle school. I wanted them to be aware we were starting with grades (since I would not see them again in a week), not harsh grading, but just an oral grade so they stayed focused and engaged in the material.

As the students answered some of my questions, I added a grade in my handwritten, not electronic, 1994 grade book. The assignment was entitled "Oral Participation" with the date at the top.

I next saw my class five days later. While calling roll, I was making sure that Robert and all my other students were present again. No answer. I asked the class where he was. They said there was no Robert. I thought they were pulling my leg, so I looked around and said, "There was a Robert last week." They all agreed that there was no such person. No Robert last week or this week. I found out they were correct.

But I was dumbfounded. I just knew I had a Robert the week before. I had a grade under "Oral Presentation" for him.

He must have been smart, because he made a 100 on that assignment.

Lip Sync

2012 Christmas CD

I was very nervous. I walked in the first time to a group of vocalists, of which I knew NO ONE. I was looking to sing again and I heard about this downtown church's all-ladies ensemble. They sang beautiful four-part harmony. But it had been 40-plus years since I had performed.

The only singing I did in that time was 1) I led some amateurs in a Sorority Greek Sing Competition in college and 2) I organized a group of ladies in my neighborhood thirty-five years later to sing carols at Christmas. That first year of our neighborhood group consisted of a soprano, an alto, and a doorbell ringer riding on a golf cart.

My neighborhood carolers added a few more vocalists over the years and sang in two-part harmony. We sounded good because the loud boom box with our instrumental Christmas music overshadowed our singing. One of the gals made a CD of our music. I've kept it in my CD collection in my bedroom and I have played it in my car every Christmas since.

We became rather popular in the neighborhood at Christmas. So popular, we ended up having to make appointments to sing our carols for neighbors during the season.

But that kind of singing was elementary compared to what I heard when I attended my first ladies ensemble group. There was a talented director who had a degree in music. And this group had been singing together for a long time.

I thought I still sounded pretty good before I went to the first practice. I mean, that's the way it sounded to me in the car…or the shower. I harmonized with the radio music and it seemed OK. I was delusional. At practice I saw how polished they were, how good their voices sounded, how well they followed the music director's instructions, and I was intimidated. BIG TIME. All those years ago, I sang first soprano, the melody. Now, I sang second soprano (harmony).

I felt overwhelmed – the new setting, the new director, the new music – and I did not really hear the person next to me to find the note I was supposed to be singing. I didn't want to make a mistake. So, I just mouthed the words. I pretended to sing. And I did it a lot. The times I knew the notes, I belted it out! The times I didn't, I stood there lip syncing. With twenty or so ladies in the ensemble, maybe I was not missed.

I wondered if my director ever knew.

CLOSET:

Excuse My French

Parlez vous, Francais?

1977 Cole-Haan shoes

My second job after college, I was hired at the Omni International Hotel as a receptionist in the Catering Department. I did all kinds of typing -just what I wanted to get out of in my first job: being a secretary. I thought I was too good for that. Those who hired me did not think that way.

I loved my first job, but was impatient. I worked as a secretary for McCann-Erickson Advertising Agency in Atlanta. McCann-Erickson was a world wide agency. We handled the Coca-Cola account and made our presence in Atlanta to be near our number one client. Our office was about a mile from the Coke offices.

I so wanted to be on the couch with the other creative people. I had taken journalism, public relations, marketing, and copywriting...everything I needed to know to get my degree. I graduated from college. I knew everything! My mother also encouraged me to take typing, and besides teaching school, that skill rewarded me with every job I applied where typing was needed.

But, impatient as I was, I gave the secretarial pool a shot. I wanted to be Peggy Olson on "Mad Men." Wasn't she promoted in the first TV season? The first season only lasted 13 weeks. I could wait that long. It did not happen.

So, I left after six months. My next job was also as a secretary. I really came up in the world, didn't I? Now I was at the Omni, greeting guests, answering phones, and typing for the Catering Department. I was professional looking in my cream and camel plaid wool skirt. I had on a light buttery frosting yellow 100% soft cotton shirt with pleats down the front which had a white collar and white cuffs. I bought it at Muse's Department Store (ladies department upstairs) at Lenox Square Mall. My camel jacket matched my skirt. I wore dark flesh colored pantyhose and my dark camel brown leather Cole-Haan shoes had a perforated toe cap and a 2" wood heel. Those shoes were so classic and I kept them for many years. But eventually, I had accumulated so many shoes in my closet that I removed them and gave them to Goodwill.

At work one day, I received a phone call from an outside line. I answered, "Hello? Omni International Catering."

"Hello. I was wondering what entree choices are being served in the main restaurant tonight."

What? She wanted me to read the entire menu? Like I had time for that? I've got to type!

"Um, hold on a minute, please. I'll have to get a menu." And I searched for one.

Since I had a deadline for my typing, I was in a real hurry as I was reading off the entrees. The main dining restaurant specialized in French cuisine. I took French in high school and college and felt I was pretty good at speaking the language. But I was in a hurry to finish my work.

I started with the hors d'ouerves and moved on to the soups and salads. Before I hit the desserts, I read the items under entrees. Reading fast and still using my best French accent, I came to one entrée that read "Trout Mariniere." Unfortunately, I had premature articulation and said, "Trout Manure."

There was silence. Then we both started howling and she said, "You have made my day."

Let's keep this French thing going

1969 Silver Charm Bracelet

I took 2 years of French in high school. We learned all that stuff about conjugation and spoke our share of rote French terminology. For instance, "Mon nom est Lee." (My name is Lee.) "Allez-vous aujourd'hui?" (How are you today?) "Parlez-vous français ?" (Do you speak French?) Over and over.

We had a French computer lab. At the front of the room there was a big control board for the teacher. The students sat behind cubicles facing the teacher and wore headsets with microphones that the teacher managed from his control panel. He listened in on us without our knowledge. He had several options of control. 1) He transferred our speaking so another student/or other students could hear. 2) He turned all the mouthpieces on at one time for the entire class to listen to each other all at once. 3) He turned all the mouthpieces on at one time so he could hear the entire class. 4) The teacher could listen in on one student at a time. This was 1968. Pretty progressive equipment.

My REDHEAD-GIRLFRIEND was in the booth next to me. That day I wore my silver charm bracelet. My charms included a cheerleading megaphone, a horse, a piano, a Bible, a musical treble cleft note, a paint brush, among others. There were about 12 charms in all. I kept that high school sterling silver bracelet in my jewelry box in my closet. But at the moment, it tickled my arm and I turned to my friend who was sitting in the booth to the right of me, slapped my arm down on her cubicle table and said, "Scratch my arm."

Well, at this moment our teacher decided to turn on the switch to have just one person's French broadcast to the entire class. And that one person was me!

And I had said, IN ENGLISH, "Scratch my arm."

The class recognized my voice and stood up looking over their booth and stared at me. My teacher was not amused.

If I was a smart French student I should have said, "Rayer mon bras."

To keep you from researching the translation, it means, "Scratch my arm."

Still more French

1950's Goren's Point Count Bidding Wheel for Bridge

I was a practical jokester. I grew up but I never stopped playing.

I tried my hand (pun intended) at bridge after I retired from teaching. Ladies in my neighborhood had a group and asked me to join and learn and I did. But I didn't learn it very well, though. It was a hard game to remember all the conventions. My mother played bridge so I looked through some of her keepsakes in my den secretary and found a GOREN Point Count Bidding Wheel that rotated for quick reference on bidding and answering a bid.

Recently, my bridge group finished for the day and everyone left the clubhouse except for four of us. On the last Wednesday of every month, we play cards and have lunch at our neighborhood clubhouse restaurant. The three other ladies and I wanted to play a few more hands. One of the gals went to the restroom before we got started. She did not take her phone with her and while she was gone, it rang.

I decided to have some fun. So, I answered it with, "Bonjour!" The person calling was one of our previous bridgettes who was trying to reach our gal in the restroom.

She said, "Oh, dear, I am so sorry. Do I have the wrong number?"

I played on as though not understanding English and said every rote sentence I learned in French class, "Parlez-vous français ? (Do you

speak French?), Comment allez-vous? (How are you?), Qu'est-ce
que vous faites ? (What are you doing?), Aujourd'hui, c'est mercredi
(Today is Wednesday), and Mon nom est Lee. (My name is Lee)."

"Oh, please, please excuse me," she begged. "I thought I was calling
my friend. I am so sorry." After her apologies, she hung up.

Well, now she thought she had the wrong number. We knew what
was going to happen next. Yep – she called back.

When she did, our friend was still not back from the ladies lounge.
I answered again, "Bonjour." Then I REPEATED everything I had
said originally, because it was about all I remembered from my high
school French days. EXCEPT this time, for some reason while she
was again apologizing, I said, "No comprende," which was Spanish.
She still didn't catch on.

Now, she was so sweet and apologetic but I thought for SURE she
would detect some Southern accent in my voice. I didn't know I was
THAT good. But she did not and again hung up so flustered, I felt
sure she thought that she was the one who made the mistake.

Our friend came back and saw us all laughing at the fact I pulled the
practical joke off twice. We caught her up on the ruse but then again
the phone rang. So SHE answered the phone, "Bonjour."

Our sweet friend started apologizing some more for her mistake, but
this time she was interrupted and was told that all was well and that
we were just having some fun with her. THEN we found out that
our perplexed gal worried when she called over and over and heard
the French language each time. She thought she made unnecessary
overseas calls and took it upon herself to call the phone company
to tell them she thought her wires were crossed and to please not
charge her for the expensive calls.

S'il Vous Plait

1982 Parisian Watercolor Paintings from Montmartre

I loved the French language. That was why I chose to take it over Spanish in high school. The spoken words were so melodic. I thought it was a very romantic language.

TIE-ONE-ONA, neighbor and friend, was a very lucky girl in her job and marriage. She was a flight attendant and her husband was an international pilot for a major airline. Before her daughter, YA, was born, she and her husband traveled extensively but traveled stand-by. That means that airline employees, including their family and friends, were able to travel often at discounted fares or free of charge. They had lower priority, typically, than regular passengers and were only allocated a seat after all passengers, who paid a regular fare, were allowed seats. Sometimes it occurred that an employee traveling standby was allowed to take his or her seat on the aircraft, only then being asked to vacate it to make way for a regular passenger.

This afforded them the opportunity to travel while they were young and childless. They went to many exotic locales. One of these trips was to Paris. I had been to Paris twice. My favorite finds were the watercolor paintings that hung in my dining room and sunroom. I bought them at Montmartre. Many artists had studios or worked in or around Montmartre. Salvador Dali, Claude Monet, Pablo Picasso, or Vincent van Gogh, were a few notables.

TIE's husband was eight years older and knew the ropes. He had tons of experience in traveling abroad. He guided his young wife through the trials and tribulations of international traveling. She had the time of her life visiting new places with his guidance.

While in Paris after visiting the tourist attractions and the out-of-the-way non-touristy venues and restaurants, they checked into their hotel for the night. Keeping costs down, the accommodations left much to be desired. The room was fine enough but the walls were paper-thin. That evening there was a party going on next door to their room and it lasted throughout the night.

Wanting to wait it out, but bone-tired, TIE and her husband were patient, at first. The occupants next door became louder and louder until TIE had enough and was about to go and tell them to keep it down. She was angry at this point and thought she would tell them off. Her husband wondered what she might do or say to get them to stop being loud.

He, being the mature traveler, said, "Let me handle this."
And so he did.

It was very late but TIE's husband was calm and collected and knew how to handle such scenarios. He walked into the hall, knocked on their neighbor's door, which the Parisian party-goers opened, and said, "SHUT THE F— UP! (pause) S'il Vous Plait.

Excusez mon français

2012 Watercolor Hostess Gift

One of my retired teacher friends (a Physical Education teacher) was a member of our retirement group of other tired teachers who once-every-other-year met at my lake house for a weekend retreat. PE-TEACHER even gave us our group name: SLUTS. It was an acronym for SOUTHERN LADIES UNDER TREMENDOUS STRESS. We were not under much stress anymore, but as teachers, we certainly had been while still teaching.

At these retreats, there were lots of good food, boat rides around the lake with our Captain (HUBBY), good conversation, lots of wine, more good conversation because of the wine, sun-tans by the pool, and memories. One of my hostess gifts was the bomb! My dearest CO-TEACHER, another member of our group, brought a watercolor picture that she painted of five Adirondack chairs sunning on the front porch of a cabin. CO-TEACHER painted each chair a different color and it was a perfect fit for my living room.

While at the pool, PE-TEACHER began a tale about one of her own children. When her oldest son was in the third grade, he had a teacher that was new to the system. She had quite a festive personality. One evening PE-TEACHER said her phone rang and it was the parent of another student who was also in her son's class.

This parent wanted to know if PE-T's son relayed any interesting information about class that day. This woman told PE-TEACHER that her own son mentioned that the new teacher "cussed" in class. After the phone call, PE-T asked her child if anything unusual had happened in class that day.

He shrugged his shoulders and said, "My teacher said she was sorry that she spoke French." In front of her students, she apparently said the word "damn" followed by the phrase, "Excuse my French."

Eh bien, je vais être damnés! (Translate it yourself.)

CLOSET

Playing Dress-up

Dick Tracy

1957 Dale Evans Cowgirl Outfit

As an only child, I entertained myself a lot.

I took piano lessons and pretended sometimes that I was the piano teacher handing out assignments. I still have this piano music where, in my childish handwriting on the music pages, I chastised my pretend student to "Pianissimo!" My pretend piano student even had a name…Becky Rogers.

I loved Roy Rogers and Dale Evans and thinking that I WAS Dale Evans as a little girl with my cowgirl outfit on, I rang my neighbor's doorbell. My friend's mother answered the door and I said, "Is Roy home? Can Roy come out to play?" "Roy" was just a year older than I. We played Roy and Dale all the time. I have that Dale Evans outfit in a box in my upstairs closet. It consisted of a solid red shirt with a plaid kerchief and a faux suede jacket with fringe. There was a round skirt and I kept a holster around my waist for my toy gun. I wore white boots that looked more like majorette boots. My cowgirl hat was tan and I wore tan gloves so I wouldn't chap my hands while riding my horse, Buttermilk. We played in my neighbor's backyard.

THE HEIR dressed up, also like me, when he was my age and in his imagination, he might be Popeye, Robin Hood, Superman or Dick Tracy. I let him wear his costumes when we were in public. People greeted him at the grocery and would say, "Hi, Superman!" or whomever he was that day.

I took THE HEIR, dressed in his Dick Tracy costume, to the city police station. When we walked inside, I looked at a lady at the front desk and nodded my head meaning "NO", and I asked her "Is Dick Tracy here?" I asked twice because at first she didn't understand my questioning. "Is Dick Tracy here?" I asked again, while I still nodded in the negative.

"Why, no, he isn't," she said, now understanding my meaning.

"But his desk is here, is that correct?" This time I nodded in the affirmative but being taller than THE HEIR, he again didn't see my gestures.

"Why, yes, it's in here," she said pointing to a closed door.

When she opened the door, there sat an empty desk with papers scattered all over it as though someone was busy at work and had to leave in a rush. I turned and said, "See, HEIR? Dick Tracy is out catching criminals and isn't at his desk. He's very busy."

So, when you are looking for something to do that doesn't cost money to entertain your four year old, take him someplace that doesn't exist and make up a story that one day you can write about or will show all your friends how foolish and silly you are.

Barbie Got Married

1961 Barbie's Wedding Dress

Who didn't have a Barbie doll in the '60's ? I had one of every hair color. Not only did I have Barbie, but I had Ken (a blonde and brunette version of him), and her cousin, Skipper. I had the Barbie casual dresses, the Barbie formal dresses, the Barbie shoes, the Barbie hats, the Barbie slacks, the Barbie swimsuits, the Barbie CAR, the Barbie board game, and the Barbie HOUSE! I was a Barbie groupie! No knock-offs. All original Barbie (made by Mattel) paraphernalia.

I loved playing Barbie so much that I wanted her to marry Ken… with a real wedding. So, naturally, I had to get the Barbie Wedding Dress! They called it "Wedding Day Barbie" and it came out in 1961. It was a silk-like full white dress with a large poof skirt. She had a flower designed taffeta overlay over the skirt and on her long sleeves. Barbie had a pearl halo-like veil made of taffeta looming large behind her hair, which did not cover her face, and she wore a pearl necklace, pearl stud earrings, white shoes, and carried a pink bouquet. After one wearing, I repackaged her dress in the Barbie cellophane front wrapped box and put it in my storage closet upstairs.

For her wedding, I invited all my friends who played with their Barbies…and, of course, their Ken dolls. My friend, THE-GIRL-I-LOOKED-UP-TO, came as did many of the girls in my neighborhood. Her mother was so sweet to offer to make the wedding cake.

It was a Barbie-and-Ken-sized 3-tier white cake with pink icing. She also made a larger one for all the guests with real pulses.

Skipper, was the Maid-of-Honor, but I don't remember what she wore. The groom, blonde Ken, looked dapper in his white-coat tuxedo. Best man, brunette Ken, did, too... like MAD MEN's Don Draper or Rock Hudson.

Well, as a matter of fact, my other blonde and brunette Barbies looked beautiful in their cocktail dresses. AND all the other attendees– those other Barbies and Kens who came - looked gorgeous, too. As a matter of fact, they all looked alike! There were no repeats in the ladies fashion, I might add. So couture! The men dolls all had on tuxes.

At the reception, the bride and groom cut the little cake and drank pink punch while the large wedding cake was served to the LIVING attendees. I took pictures with my 960 Kodak Brownie Cresta 3 Camera which used 120 film and produced 6 x 6 images. Barbie and Ken left in her pink convertible. I developed the pictures and made Barbie and Ken a wedding album, which is with Barbie's wedding dress.

When they returned after the honeymoon (they did not tell me where they went), they lived in Barbie's pink cardboard-papered house and still drove her convertible all over my living room rug.

Poor Ken was always in that pink car.

Hip-Hip-Hooray

1956 High School Yearbook

I loved my cheerleading experience. From my very first memory all the way through college, I enjoyed cheering. I was 3 years old and did not realize until later when I saw pictures of myself that my first memory was as a mascot for the cheerleading squad of my small town's high school. In my first memory I sat Indian style on the ground with the sun shining on my face. I didn't know what or why I was sitting there until years later, when seeing a 1956 yearbook in the storage closet that belonged to my mother, I knew that was the moment.

In that picture I had on a darling black wool skirt with shoulder straps buttoned at the waist. The skirt had three little puppies of various sizes appliquéd on it. I wore a white short sleeve cotton shirt with a Peter Pan collar. I had a red cardigan sweater and wore white socks with red Keds. Red and black were our school colors.

Later I cheered in high school. It was just a popularity contest. We weren't judged by ability, we were judged by the student body's votes. Luckily, we were all good enough and eventually, the summer before my Senior year, we won the SPIRIT STICK for best squad at the 1970 NCA CHEER CLINIC camp. The 1970's were a juxtaposition of the old-school cheers to the beginning of the new cheerleading styles today. We were doing back flips, round-offs (gymnastic moves), and even without male cheerleaders, we performed shoulder stands.

While Seniors, our skirts shortened a foot from my Freshman cheering days. We bridged a gap from old to new in those four years I cheered in high school…1967-1971.

Although we had modern cheers to go along with our gymnastic moves, we still carried on the tradition of our tried-and-true cheers.

Some of our old cheers consisted of these:

"2-bits, 4-bits, 6-bits, a dollar! All for (team name), stand up and holler!"

"2-4-6-8 – Who do we appreciate? (team name here)"

"Hey, hey, whatdaya say? Take the ball the other way!" (basketball cheer)

"Look at the scoreboard. What do you find? We're not losing, We're just behind!"

We didn't really cheer that last one. I read it somewhere. I just had to add it.

How the school got away with our fight song for as long as it did, I'll never know. It was sung before I got there and long after I left. The music was the Notre Dame Fight Song. Here are the words:

> "Beer, Beer for 'ole _____(school name) High,
> You bring the whiskey, I'll bring the rye.
> Send Mr./Mrs. _____(favorite teacher), out for gin,
> Don't let a soul but a _____(Senior, Junior, etc.) in.
> We never stagger, we never fall,
> We sober up on wood alcohol,
> When we yell, we yell like hell,
> For the glory of _____(school name) High."

Unbelievable.

"When I grow up, I want to be..."

1991 Robin Hood Outfit

My first degree in college was in print journalism and public relations. I took marketing classes and public speaking. I made promos for our college radio station. My second degree in grad school was Secondary English Education. I taught English, a core subject in every high school, but one school had us also teaching elective classes. Mine was Mass Media. This included journalism, radio, television, and cinema. I always liked movies, so it was fun to teach the history of the medium. From my childhood to my eldest son's childhood, much had changed in film in many areas, but especially with special effects: more intensity, reality, and gore.

I took The HEIR to the theater at a young age, but felt that if I explained away the PG-13 scenes, he wouldn't be scared and he would have seen how special effects worked. He was seven when I took him to see "Robin Hood, Prince of Thieves" with Kevin Costner, Morgan Freeman, and Sean Connery.

We knew the Robin Hood story. But this was the movie everyone made fun of because Kevin Costner couldn't keep his English accent for the entire movie. Sometimes he said a line in a British accent, then later, he did not, but they filmed it anyway. It made quite a running joke about his performance.

I LOVED the parody to this movie by Mel Brooks, "Robin Hood,

Men in Tights." Sir Robin, played by Carey Elwes, answered a question in the movie about why he was such a good archer and he answered, "Because I can speak with a real British accent." (Elwes was from England and you might remember him as being the prince in "The Princess Bride.")

As the action scenes heated up, I leaned over whispering to my oldest about how this or that wasn't real. I said, "Do you ever see something like this in REAL life?" The HEIR answered, "No." I mean I dissected all the intense fighting scenes which accentuated the play acting.

As we left the movie theater, The HEIR looked up to me and said, "I now know who I want to be when I grow up!"

I thought after seeing that fantastic archer, Robin of Loxley, aka Robin Hood, he was the man! Robin Hood was fierce, had no fear, and a forest warrior! I thought this was a good sign that he related to the hero. I knew he was interested in Robin Hood because he dressed up and played Robin Hood around the house. His bedroom closet stored his Robin Hood felt green costume with the Kelly green felt pointed hat that had a fake ostrich feather attached. He tied an orange felt sash to his tunic. We bought a cape to tie around his shoulders. We found brown boots that he wore to complete the look.

I still asked, "Who is it you want to be?"

His answer? "Kevin Costner."

Never in a million years did I think he wanted to be the actor.

Going AWOL

1993 Military School Application Brochures

With a first child, we didn't know what we were doing. I wasn't a good disciplinarian because I wasn't disciplined all that much. The only reason I tried to behave was not to disappoint my mother. The look on her face was enough to tow the line. She could have been a travel agent for guilt trips. I was strong-willed and was tough to handle, unless I wanted to please or not feel guilty.

Even for the most part The HEIR was easy to raise, however, we did have our moments. I tried to slough off my parental responsibilities on to others. When The SPARE was a toddler, I told him The White Police, The Brown Police, and The Red Police were watching at all times. Riding in the car, if a white police car drove by on the roads (the city police), I pointed them out. I did the same with The Brown Police (county deputies in brown cars). It was hard to find The Red Police without it being a fire truck or emergency vehicle. But occasionally, there would be a red truck with a light on the roof. And when I did find one, I made sure I pointed it out to him.

If we ate lunch or dinner out, I said that there could be red, white, or brown police dining all around us and if he misbehaved while were dining out or if some restaurant patron told the police about his poor behavior, there was nothing I could do. I never said what would happen. I left that up to his imagination.

I was in the same mindset with our first son. Around the end of the elementary school years, there was a contest of wills between him and us. I did not want to deal with it. Hubby worked more and more and I seemed to have to handle a lot of the home stuff.

I wrote to several military boarding schools in Georgia and Alabama. Over the next week, I received lots of pamphlets describing their schools and how they could whip rascally boys into fine young men. Their brochures had beautiful pictures. They came with testimonials, mottos, school objectives, and history of their institution. They all sounded great. And they were all pricey.

We were not going to send him away. But I didn't tell him that. I just wanted to scare him a little so that he would comply with our household rules. I took ALL the brochures and scattered them neatly across the kitchen table as though I had been perusing them. My objective was for him to see them and be nervous.

When he walked in the kitchen, he saw them, glanced over the material, turned to me and asked, "You can wear uniforms at these schools?" (He grew up loving to wear costumes, remember.)

I answered, "Yes."

"And you get to carry a gun?"

"I think so," I was feeling nervous with this line of questioning.

"Then, sign me up!"

Why did most of my antics backfire on me and why did I still keep those stupid pamphlets in cardboard boxes in my hall closet? Oh, yes, I remember…in case they worked for round two eight years later.

CLOSET:

Claim to Fame

Kissing Cuzins

1971 Bass Saddle Oxford Shoes

I've been kissed by a President. Yup. You read that correctly.

After high school graduation and before attending college, I didn't have a summer job. I tried to enjoy those last free days before leaving home. That summer of 1971, I volunteered to help my county's Chamber of Commerce participate in the STAY AND SEE GEORGIA campaign.

The Georgia Department of Industry, Trade, and Tourism planned celebration activities at Lenox Square Mall (which in 1971 was an open air mall with breezeways connecting the stores). They planned to bring together partners in Georgia's tourism industry to showcase Georgia's assets and spread a message of "Stay and See Georgia." Don't spend your travel dollars elsewhere. Stay and see what Georgia offers.

The campaign was one week long and several of us who were YOUNG GIRLS manned the booth for our county. We wore our high schools' matching cheerleading outfits so we would all look uniformed. The uniform top was a solid red vest with an Oxford cloth white Peter Pan collared shirt, which the length of the sleeves came to our elbow. We had on white knee socks with still-in-my-closet Bass Saddle Oxford shoes. The knee socks had a tassel at the fold at the top. The skirt was mighty short. It was only as long as your fingertips by your side. The uniform had a red and black pleated plaid skirt for our school colors.

Our county's treasure that we promoted was the Monastery of the Holy Spirit. This tourist attraction had individuals of all faiths flock to the monastery. The beautiful 2,100 acres was a popular spot for picnics, strolls, perusing the Gift Shop, and enjoying the Bonsai nursery. One experienced this serenity of restful recollection and spiritual renewal retreat for a day, or as long as a week.

This was, mainly, all our county was known for. Sometimes you heard, "Oh, I go through your county on my way to Athens." And years later, we heard "Eat, Drink, and See Mary!" – a slogan assigned to bumper stickers regarding the lady who was a self-proclaimed visionary of the Mother Mary. She announced her next "vision" day and people started coming across the globe to hear what she claimed Mary had told her. She emerged from her home where thousands converged. Boy, was this good for businesses…

But in 1971 we finished our week chatting with buyers at the mall and handing out brochures of information. It came to a climax when the Governor's Mansion held a reception for all participants. They feted us to munchies and punch for our week of hard work. We also stood in the receiving line to meet and thank our host and hostess, the Georgia governor and his wife.

Telling my aunt about our upcoming reception, she mentioned we were related (in the South we call it kin) to Jimmy Carter. I had no fear of speaking in public. While in college, I changed my major to Public Relations. While in line, I approached the couple. I shook Rosalyn's hand first and then when I was in front of the governor, I said, "My aunt researched our family tree and found out we are cousins." I moved on to the next person to shake his hand.

From my peripheral vision, I saw Jimmy Carter leaning in closer to me and then he planted a big kiss on my cheek and said, "I always kiss my cousins!"

Telling this story years later in the late 1980's and 1990's to a classroom full of high school students, I prefaced my story with "I have been kissed by a President."

Their response? "Who was it? Bill Clinton?"

Speaking of Beer

*1978 Pappagallo Bahama Pink Monogrammed
Interchangeable Cover Purse*

When I was a Senior in college, I was enrolled in a university not far
from the Atlantic Ocean beaches.

That Fall, my parents drove over to my school to pick me up and
then take me out for a weekend in Hilton Head, S.C. Hilton Head
was known for its golf courses and resort. Daddy TRIED to teach
me to play golf while I was in high school and we played a few times
at our county country club, but I was stubborn and never really listened to his advice. I just wanted to play and learn. Not learn and
play.

While in Hilton Head, he took me out for a round of golf. We headed over to Harbor Town Golf Course and signed up to play 18 holes.
Because we were a twosome, the golf pro asked would we mind playing as a foursome with another gentleman and his son. Daddy said,
"No, we don't mind."

We teed off. I was terrible. But the son was really good. So good, in
fact, daddy got lots of information about his playing. He was a senior at the University of Texas and after graduation he wanted to play
on the pro tour. My father thought, "I am going to remember this
young man's name." And his name was BEN CRENSHAW.

I played golf with Ben Crenshaw. But he wasn't the Ben Crenshaw we see today or the announcers' label, "Gentle Ben." This guy reminded me of the Pillsbury Doughboy. He had that mane of great blonde hair but was as round as Humpty Dumpty. He was not the looker we would eventually see on TV. No matter, for several years I told everyone I had played golf with Ben.

I played golf terribly but I still loved the game and loved watching it and I was a great golf groupie. During my teaching years, I rounded up my other teacher girlfriends for road trips during our Spring breaks . Most people my age headed to the beach with their hard bodies to view other hard bodies. NOT ME! I talked my friends into going to Hilton Head to see the cute golfers. For several years, this was our Spring Break destination.

One of those years, my girlfriends and I became separated while following some Wake Forest golfers and I was walking alone near the clubhouse trying to find my fellow educators. Tipsy from beer, I wandered around looking for my friends.

Then, I saw a familiar face. As it approached, I was excited to see someone I knew! It was Ben Crenshaw and his entourage. I yelled out, in my confused state, "Hey! Ben!"

He stopped. And his entourage stopped with him.

What had I just done?

I was 25. I was young. And I wore a short floral pink golf skirt by Lily Pulitzer. I had on my Kelly green Pappagallo flats with a brass buckle over the top. I wore a sleeveless collared Polo shirt. Since it was April, I had on a matching green cardigan sweater in case the weather cooled later in the day.

My watch band was grosgrain pink and green. I carried my interchangeable Pappagallo Bahama pink purse (which I continued to keep with my other closet purses – just in case I bring it out again!)

that had my initials monogrammed in the same Kelly green as my shoes. My long blonde hair was held back with a pink hair band. I was already tan from lying out on warm weekends in Atlanta (but with all the colors, I looked like a fruit bowl).

I stammered, "I played golf with you here a few years ago."

Ben said, "Oh, yeah? Is that right?"

"No, really. My dad and I played with you and your dad."

"Are you sure it wasn't Tom Kite?" (Now, don't ask me why the television announcers used to confuse those two except they both played for the University of Texas.) I am sure I would have remembered."

I thought, you know, he doesn't remember and I wanted to make sure he KNOWS I am not just talking smack. I did play with him. And to prove it, I needed to mention something that would jog his memory.

So, I said, "Oh, no. It was you because you were FAT then!"

There was mild laughter from the group that followed him and then he quietly and humbly said, "Yeah. I was."

"Don't Cry for me, Argentina"

1973 letter from the Director of the Office of Management and Budget
Reagan Administration

My mother used to share this story. She taught for 37 years to all types of IQ's and personalities. In the 1950's, students were lumped into the same classroom. High achievers. Slugs. All kinds.

During this decade, she had several outstanding students. One of her students had eventual influence on the national level. My county only had ONE white high school as we were segregated during this time. You may have heard his name in the political arena over the years. Eventually we had several more famous people who graduated from this small county. There was an Oscar winner, pro football athletes, a Pulitzer Prize winner, and other famous celebrities who originated from my Smalltown, Georgia. Mother had retired by the time the other eventually- famous students were in school. But this one outstanding student kept in touch, in a way, with my mother long after he graduated from high school.

Looking back through her old yearbooks, which I kept in my guest room's closet, I saw she had her picture taken one year in a dress that I remembered she wore the most often. It was a grey-green light weight wool jacket with matching pencil skirt falling just below the knee. Her jacket had lapels and she wore it over a white polyester sleeveless shell blouse. Her only jewelry was her earrings and her Timex 2Tone Classic Expansion Stretch Band Dress Watch and earrings. They were gold-plated clip-on that looked like leaves. She wore flesh colored hose attached to her girdle and on her feet were brown leather pumps with two-inch heels.

One day mother taught a lesson about Argentina's government and Juan Peron, the Argentine General and politician who was elected three times as President of Argentina. He was overthrown in a military coup in 1955. Mother casually mentioned to her class, "Mark my words. Peron will be back."

This gifted, young student must have taken her words to heart. He graduated from high school and earned his B.B.A. in Economics from the University of Georgia in 1964. He became an assistant professor of Economics at Georgia State University. He later earned his Ph.D. in Economics in 1969 from the University of Virginia. As wonderful as this career seems, his star was still rising.

This young man's name was James C. Miller, III. In July 1985, President Ronald Reagan chose this "conservative economist who favors reducing the size of the federal government" as his administration's new budget director. Yes, our little Jimmy Miller who sat in our small school's government class.

Before his rise in the Reagan administration and his movement up this brilliant career ladder, he must not have forgotten his high school roots and his Government teacher. When Peron returned to power in 1973 (although briefly, as he served for nine months until his death in 1974 only to be succeeded by his third wife), Jimmy wrote a letter to my mother, which she kept with other cards and letters that I now have, about this event.

Sometimes as teachers, we seldom know what influence we had on our students when they become adults. My mother probably taught that Argentine lesson hundreds of times and didn't remember her own exact words when she taught Jimmy Miller but he did.

His letter to her was brief. All it said was:

"Mrs. Archer,

You were right. Peron's back."

- Jimmy Miller

What's in a Name?

1970 – Music Composers' Busts

I loved my piano teacher when I took private lessons in high school. She was youthful and very talented. She was also at one time, Georgia's "Junior Miss." I thought that was awesome. Today they call the pageant Distinguished Young Women.

She had a very unique name, in my opinion. I liked it, too. It was traditionally unique. Was that an oxymoron? Her name was Mary John.

I took piano lessons for nine years. That was a lot of practicing. As a teenager, I played very mechanically and hit most of my notes. Today, I play with years of life experience and with feeling, but accuracy? Not so much.

I didn't know it at the time, but this was going to be my last year taking piano lessons. I was going to concentrate on singing girls' trio, girls' ensemble, choir, and solo performances at my high school and church. I guess I was OK, because I was asked to sing in two weddings while in high school and I did participate in the high school state Literary Meets, winning my district and going to state in girls' trio and girls' solo.

I was in the 11th grade when I sat on her bench and finished my piano piece. I was memorizing my music for the National Playing Piano Auditions. Every year her students performed music for this guild and after doing so, we received a certificate with our names in calligraphy for our efforts. Whoopee.

My music teacher gave each of us a 4" high bust of a famous composer for all the effort we put into memorizing two musical pieces. When I became old enough to participate in the guild, I received seven statues over the nine years: Strauss, Beethoven, Bach, Chopin, Haydn, Brahms, and Mozart. They were alabaster off-white with each composer's name etched on their busts. It was nerve-wracking to perform, but I sure did appreciate my collection. Those seven composers were placed on my piano and haven't moved.

She sat beside me in a chair with her spiral notebook in hand to take notes on my weekly piano performance. Somehow we began talking about her unique name. She had a girl/boy name. I hadn't known anyone before with that combination.

She said she was named for both her parents. Cool. But the most interesting part about her name was when she was in the first grade, she was the only double-named girl in her class because the rest of the girls in her entire class were named MELANIE. And they were named MELANIE because the book and movie, "Gone With the Wind" was so popular. All the mothers wanted their daughters to be like Melanie Wilkes.

Besides, having an unusually pretty name, along with being a superb pianist, helped this Georgia's Junior Miss stand out in the America's Junior Miss Pageant.

Broadway Joe

1971 College Scrapbook

In my small town, there was a wonderful gentleman who owned a five-and-ten variety store. The high school seniors leaving for college for the first time were the recipients of his generosity. He pulled together a collection of items from his store, packaged them, and mailed them to the college freshman a few weeks after the university school year started. It made us feel at home in case we were homesick. Very sweet.

The package contained all kinds of goodies from his store: fireballs, wax bottles with a Kool-aid type colored drink, Bit O'Honey candy, gum, pencils, erasers, spiral notebooks, those big red wax lips, and such. Mine came within the first month of school. The box was wrapped in brown paper with string tied around it. Since I did not know about this hometown gentleman doing this for incoming freshmen and only found out later he had been doing this for many years, I was confused about this arrival. On the return address of my package it read, "Joe Willie Namath. Shapula, Mississippi." Was there a Shapula, Mississippi?

I brought the package back from the mailroom to my dorm and began opening it in the community area on my hall. In 1971, we lived in dorms that had two girls to a room, community bathrooms and showers for the girls on the floor, and a community living room for the entire hall. The living room had one TV and you had better get used to sharing it. And there was only one phone for all the girls. Get used to that, too.

My roommate and I knew each other in high school. We had the most fun decorating our room with coordinating bedspreads and pillows. She loved daisies and our room was all yellow and white, very bright and clean looking. We had bulletin boards along the side of our single beds, which pulled out for sleeping, but pushed back against the wall to also act as a sofa. The side of the bed was padded and opened up from bottom to top like on the airplanes to store your luggage.

I kept and cherished the many mementos in my guest bedroom closet scrapbooks from my bulletin boards: theatre programs, cards from one college boyfriend who sent flowers for some reason or other, ticket stubs for baseball games from another boyfriend who played college baseball, letters from my mother, dead corsages with wrinkled ribbons from dances, and more.

While opening the package that arrived that day, my next door dorm neighbor was in the room. She asked who it was from. I told her what it read on the return address and then had an idea! I decided to ride this wave of a practical joke as long as I could.

I lied, "I met Joe Namath last year in New York City, but I never expected this!"

Astonishment! She bought it! She said, "You KNOW Joe Namath? How did you meet him?"

"Well, my dad, as a coach (true), was asked to attend this national coach's conference in New York and mother and I tagged along (not true). The guest speaker was Joe Namath. After his speech, I went up to him, like dozens of others, and told him I enjoyed his speech. We started talking and we wrote a few times, but I never thought I'd receive a gift from him." She bought it.

So to keep up the ruse throughout the year, when Broadway Joe was on TV in a commercial for L'eggs Pantyhose, or Noxema's "take it off" shaving cream commercials, I threw in my ammunition, "Joe likes the color blue", or "Joe enjoys pizza", and other lies to build my case.

Near the end of the school year, surprisingly, I received another package from the Variety Store Owner. My dorm neighbor saw that I had another one and jealously asked, "Who is it from? JOE NAMATH?"

I started confessing! I couldn't let her go back home for the summer with my lie. "I can't believe it!" she said. "I went back to Savannah and told everyone I know that I have a friend who knows Joe Namath!"

Well, it should end there. But the practical joke made it back to my hometown and the local newspaper wrote about it. Not a lot of real news happened that week, I supposed. Then the "Atlanta Constitution" (now the "Atlanta Journal/Constitution") picked up that story and wrote about it on their editorial page.

Since the AJC was a state-wide paper, luckily for my blonde Savannah friend, they didn't use our real names.

I See Dead People

2000 Picture Frames

While teaching high school, I tried to create a room that was cozy. I felt students learned best in a comfortable environment. If students and teachers spent almost as much or more time in their day at their job/school than their own home, then I was hoping my government-built-public-classroom felt like home away from home as much as possible.

I added big and little lamps to spread out the light rather than just having the overhead florescent lighting. I brought appropriate hanging pictures and placed posters regarding my literary subject around the room. Along the wall-long cabinets were shelves. I added books, pictures of travel places, and my family photos.

Besides my family, I had photos of famous people that I admired. While teaching in 2000, I wasn't quite over Princess Diana's and John-John Kennedy's deaths. So, on a separate shelf, I placed their pictures in frames that I recycled from my storage closet.

These two photographs came from my home, where for a while they decorated a drop leaf table in my den along with family and friends' pictures. Jack Nicklaus was added to the mix, too. HUBBY lived in California for a time and played Pebble Beach Golf Club a few times, but as he watched the Pebble Beach Pro-Am from the gallery, he was able to take a great close-up picture of the "Golden Bear."

These framed photographs of the celebrities held a special place in my heart. Once a gal came to my house and perused my dozens of pictures on the table when her eyes stopped and stared at the JFK, Jr. photograph and she said, "This person sure does look familiar."

Uh, yeah.

Eventually I added Tim Matheson to the collection (Otter from "Animal House.") NANNOO, an Atlanta running mate, knew how much I lusted after him for years and when I became engaged, she wrote him to tell him so that possibly he might write back with "Best Wishes." This wasn't schoolgirl crush stuff. We were pushing 30. However, he did not write back.

Since I tried to decorate my classroom comfortably, I took Princess Di and John-John's pictures and placed them on a separate book-shelf. A student came up one day and said to me while pointing to those two, "Mrs. St. John, why do you have those pictures in your room?"

I explained how I adored them before they died and just wanted to have their picture around because they meant so much to me at one time and died too soon.

He then said, "Well, don't go putting my picture on your shelf because all you've got up there are DEAD PEOPLE."

Same Song…

2010 Pearl Necklace

In 2010, I was invited to my past employer's Class of 2000's Ten-Year High School Reunion where I taught British and American Literature. It was great seeing all those guys. I dressed up for this event. I had on Jones of New York black dress slacks with Etienne Aigner polka dot pumps. I wore a solid matching black ¾ length sleeve pull-over knit with a boat neck and a big round embroidered collar that I bought at Belk's. I wore my single pearl earrings and my pearl necklace with a diamond and sapphire clasp. I bought a safe for all my mother's jewels and a few of mine that I didn't wear all that much, like my necklace. I kept the safe in my closet for many years.

These former students had many accomplishments in the 10 years after high school. I was proud of them and enjoyed seeing each and every one. Later, I really enjoyed living vicariously through one of my students, Elizabeth Cauvel, who competed on 2014 "Master Chef". She was the runner-up that season. She should have won.

At the reunion, one student came up to me and told me, "TO THIS DAY, I still quote you." That was flattering but I thought, "Oh, no. What did I say that would make someone want to reuse stuff I said?" So, I asked.

He said, "It was the quote you always told us: 'I'm sorry. I didn't mean to be talking while you were interrupting.' "

Great line. I used it a lot when I was trying to get my Seniors' attention. Administrators told us not to use sarcasm in the classroom, but that one was just too good to pass up. I don't remember who I stole it from because I certainly didn't make it up.

The thing about that line was that the 2000 teaching year wasn't the first time I used it. I taught in every decade since the 1970's until 2009. Not every year of every decade, just every decade. (If I had stayed one year longer, I could have said, "I taught in five decades and I am only 56." – the age I retired).

I used that line, "Excuse me. I didn't mean to be talking while you are interrupting" in every one of them...the 70's, the 80's, the 90's, and the 00's. However, the reactions were different.

In the late 1970's and early 1980's, when my students went off- topic too much and started conversations of their own about anything else but the subject at hand, I'd say that line and their response was, "Oh, Mrs. St. John. We are sooooooo sorry." And they stopped talking at that very moment. In the 1990's, when I said it, the response then was "Oh, Mrs. St. John, we're sorry. But they talked a little more before settling down. By the 2000's, it was "Oh." And they kept on talking until I had to try something else.

I had some great classes and this wasn't the general rule, but it did happen. Now I know why our parents would say in front of us, "What is happening to this new generation? No respect for authority."

I got it.

Little Miss Dynamite

1958 Pink Autograph Book

Her songs were hits in the 1950's and 1960's. "Rocking Around The Christmas Tree" was probably one of her most well-known. And I was introduced to her but didn't remember that I did. It was my mother who told me about meeting her. And she was proud of my behavior, too.

At one-time, Brenda Lee, lived in my small town. My parents' neighborhood friend had once taught her in first grade, I think. But she moved to the adjoining town soon after that and she only came back when visiting her grandmother, who still lived in my small town on a street between two churches.

After she moved away she became famous. She was born Brenda Mae Tarpley in 1944 and was the top-charting female vocalist of the 1960's. She sang country, pop, and rockabilly music. She was ranked fourth in the decade for her 47 U.S. chart hits during the '60's and only surpassed by Elvis, The Beatles, and Ray Charles. She was best known for her 1960's hit "I'm Sorry" and for her 1958 hit "Rocking Around The Christmas Tree." "Rocking Around the Christmas Tree" was a holiday standard. She received the nickname, Little Miss Dynamite, in 1957 because of her small frame, only 4' 9", and after she recorded the song, "Dynamite." She was one of the earliest pop stars to have a major contemporary international following.

As fans, my ALMOST- BIG- SISTER, her mother (Brenda's former first grade teacher), my mother and I knew she was visiting her grandmother and asked to come by and meet her. I was 5 years old in 1958 and it was a big year for her. She was 14. My ALMOST-BIG- SISTER was 8 and we were so excited to meet this star!

Wearing a solid red circle skirt with a white blouse and black cable cardigan sweater with white socks and black leather Mary Jane shoes, I carried my little autograph book and pen with me up to her grandmother's front porch. My book was made of pink plastic and had a design of a young girl with a blonde ponytail holding her own collection of autograph books. The pages inside of this little six-by-four-and-a-half-inch book were multi-colored. It had solid pastel pink, white, yellow, green, and blue pages, which people chose to write upon. In the back were a few stiff black pages so photos could be added. It stayed a part of my collection of memories in my storage room closet.

All four of us climbed the steps to her grandmother's door at the chosen time to visit. Mother rang the doorbell and we waited…for quite a while. Finally, Brenda Lee's grandmother opened the door and apologized for making us wait. She asked us to wait another moment as she had to go to the back of the house. Although she knew we were coming by and maybe knew we were waiting as fans on her grandmother's porch, Brenda Lee was taking her sweet time to come to the door. She had fallen asleep, her grandmother said. Brenda didn't want to be awakened from her nap.

Mother said when she finally made her entrance, my ALMOST-BIG-SISTER and I put our little autograph books behind our backs and didn't ask her for her signature.

I guess we knew poor behavior when we saw it, even then.

What is it with Presidents and us?

1990 Pirate Outfit

Mother was a high school government teacher. Always reading history, she stayed current with world news, although she mostly read about the English Royal Families.

She and my dad talked politics at the dinner table and by osmosis, I picked up a few names in their conversation. She employed a couple of her very reliable high school female students to baby sit me occasionally. They wanted to find out how smart I might be as a teacher's child and one night they asked, "Who is President of the United States?" They were flabbergasted when I answered, "Eisenhower."

That's all it took for them to think I was exceptional.

When our oldest was five in 1990, George Herbert Walker Bush was in the White House. And for some reason, he wanted to invite him to his upcoming birthday party. So, we made up his birthday invitations and found out where the Republican Party headquarters in our town was, went there, and handed a party invitation to one of the leading Republican Party's promoters. In front of my child, the gentleman said he would try to make sure the president received it.

A few weeks later yet before the party, The HEIR received a package from Washington, D.C. and in it was a beautiful glossy picture book of the interior rooms of the White House. He was a little sad that he didn't hear from the president directly and that he had no official word as to whether the President was coming to his party.

We had the party. It was a pirate party. The guests wore costumes and there were treasure maps which were burned on the edges of the paper to make it look old. The maps showed where there were hidden treasures in our yard and we asked our friends' middle school children to lead the hunt of the teams of 5-year-old birthday guests to their quests. Each map directed the party-goers to different locations around our property and whoever got to the treasure site first, found the stash, and brought it back to the outdoor picnic table, won more prizes for their group. Our son's black and white pirate costume with a red swashbuckling sash, the puffy white long-sleeve shirt, the eye patch, the sword, and the black felt hat with a white feather was a hit. I never found a better place to keep it but on hanger in storage.

George Herbert Walker Bush did not show up. Arrggghhh!

I knew that picture book was all he would receive for his birthday but appreciated the man at the Republican headquarters taking that little invitation to the next level. A week later, I called a family friend and asked him to pretend he was the President and to speak to our oldest to tell him "in person" that he was unable to attend.

Our friend did call and asked to speak to The HEIR. When our five-year-old answered the phone he heard, "This is President Bush. I am sorry I was unable to come to your party. There was so much going on in the country and the world. I was busy…uh, being, uh… presidential."

'nuff said.

CLOSET:

Making the Grade

Testing, Testing

2000 Florida State University Hoodie

When THE HEIR was in the 8th grade, the counselors gave his class an aptitude test to gain insight into the kinds of jobs students could be thinking about for their futures. They gave the test before high school so that pupils could plan on what courses they should take for either the college-prep course track diploma or the technical track diploma.

Now THE HEIR was an exceptional student. He might even be considered a "student athlete." He later captained his Varsity Football team, was selected All-Region in his football position by the metropolitan newspaper in our state, and took AP and Joint Enrollment courses. Universities came knocking and offered around $180,000 of academic scholarship to him his Junior and Senior years and plenty of football scholarships as well.

By the time he was a Senior, he wore the same uniform to school every day. It consisted of a burgundy pull-over hoodie with "Florida State Seminoles" in gold letters stitched on the back. I had to keep up with the wash so he'd have that pull-over ready for school each day. He wore it with black or grey painter's pants, Croc shoes, and white ankle socks. Fall – hoodie/painter's pants; Winter – hoodie/painter's pants; and Spring – hoodie/painter's pants. By Spring, he might wear sandals. Why was that hoodie still here in his bedroom closet? It should have been thrown away.

But in 8th grade we waited to know the results of this aptitude test. When they came in, his tests said he was good with his hands (and he did major in Information Technology- so they got that part right) and the results encouraged him to become either a butcher or an air-conditioner repairman.

Nothing wrong with those jobs, but his tenacity to work with computers was certainly more futuristic!

However, the real clincher was what the girl next to him in class received on her test results. They told her she should either become a clown or a mime.

What?

Wonder what became of her?

And THE HEIR? Not working in the meat department. Currently working on his M.B.A.

My Friend Flicka

1960 Breyer Horse Collection

I loved horses growing up. In the 1960's, I owned individual and sets of the Breyer Horse Collections. These play horses were glossy plastic. I had the Arabian family set, a 6 ½" foal, the 8 ¾" mare, and the 9 ¼" stallion. Not only Arabian, I had the Palaminos, Apaloosas, Quarterhorses, and Clydesdale varieties. I placed duct tape on the bottom of my horses' bellies and wrote their names to help me remember who was who. The Stallion I owned was named KING. The baby? FLAME. I kept them in the playroom closet for years for my boys. Those horses were used for 2 generations.

As an only child with my overactive imagination to entertain myself on long road trips, I cracked the backseat window (where I always had to sit since my parents occupied the front seats) and pretended I was holding on to a leash that reigned in my horse who was running along side our car for hours at a time. Poor horse. Sometimes he ran 60 miles per hour for 3 hours at a time down the expressway. New meaning for horsepower. I held my hand out the window with no problems because we never wore seat belts in the 1960's.

My cousin had a horse once. I watched it bite her on the cheek when I was young. That's one probable reason my parents never got one for me and because they knew my cousins wouldn't mind if I rode hers instead. Another childhood friend had two horses in her backyard within the city limits. That was allowed in my small town. I rode with her some.

In third grade, a group of girls (never boys) played "horse" at recess. We pretended to ride horses over jumps in the school yard. We pulled broken branches and gathered rocks from the playground to build low-jumping fences all over the school yard. Recess must have been an hour because EVERY DAY it took that long to rebuild our horse jump area. By the time we finished building and were ready to jump, we'd have about 5 minutes left at recess and then we'd be called in to come to class.

Next day, same thing because the fourth graders came to recess after us and tore down all our hard work. I guess those fourth graders didn't like playing "horses." We built them all back up, jumped for bit, then we were called to come back because recess was over. It was like the movie, "Ground Hog Day." We built, we jumped, we left, then torn down. Built, jumped, left, torn down. Why did we continue to put up with that?

But what else were we gonna do? All we had on our playground were swings. We had mastered that. And we weren't going to play with the boys. They had imaginary guns.

Behave Yourself
2003 Scrapbook Craft Stickers

I tried; believe me I really did. Growing up, I felt confined when I adhered to rules. I tried to behave, but sometimes it was just my nature to be out of control. Would it be called an artist's temperament?

I tried to get organized as an adult and set a good example. Life was full – baseball practices, school, piano lessons, scouts, and church activities. I thought if I set up a behavior/organizational chart, it helped both The HEIR and ME to get organized. If there was a chart in his bathroom, like a calendar, he saw what his short-term future was, for at least a week, and knew how to plan to get homework assignments done or get to bed at a decent time. Then came his rewards and he would be proud of himself. We included rewards like stickers, stars, candy treats and privileges. I could be proud of me, too, as I was determined to get our lives systemized. It lasted two weeks.

For one week, I tried to follow-through with doing things on a set schedule. I tried to remember to put stickers, etc., for accomplishments. I may have done things for rewards as a child, but my parents didn't set a chart for me to observe and follow. I just behaved, even as a free-spirit. I felt guilty when I didn't. My mother knew how to lay the guilt trips on me. As a matter of fact, she could lay those guilt trips on me (travel agent for guilt trips, remember?) It worked on me and that was the only reason I towed the line.

When it came time for The SPARE to be under rule with charts and graphs, I just didn't even attempt it. His fourth grade teacher encouraged me in a parent conference one time to set one up and I just looked at her and said, "I can't."

She looked puzzled.

"What do you mean, you can't?" she asked.

And then I explained the first scenario with our first child and how it didn't work, not so much for him, but for me, and that I had always wondered what kind of example was I setting if my children saw that I had set goals of some kind and couldn't follow through. I thought that display would be worse. Do as I say, not as I do? What kind of example is that?

And so guess what I didn't do? I kept the unused stickers in my craft drawer if anyone wants them.

CLOSET:

Marriage Vows

As Lewis Grizzard Said...

1983 Couture Fashion Designers

Lewis Grizzard was one of my favorite writers. When I first taught high school in the late 1970's, I read his Atlanta Journal/Constitution columns aloud every morning to my students before I started teaching my classes. Somewhere I read that if you started the day off with humor, you would get your brain flowing.

He was married four times. Something he said around wife two or maybe three, stuck with me. "We've been married for 6 weeks and they said it wouldn't last." It was about six weeks into my marriage that I felt like leaving my husband.

My husband and I, like my parents, married at 30. We enjoyed our 20's immensely and felt like we got all the playing out of us before settling down. It was a rite of passage. What we didn't expect was that we were also set in our ways.

What I loved about my husband when we met was that he wasn't like my father. Oh, he had all the wonderful traits of my dad, but I wasn't going to baby my husband the way my mother babied my father. (Or so I thought).

What I saw in dating, I thought would last. It was my first visit to his newly purchased home, which he bought as a bachelor, where I happily discovered that he ironed, cooked a little, and did laundry, etc. Loved it! On the first date we had in his home, he cooked steaks on the grill, made a salad, and baked potatoes in the microwave. He cleared the table, cleaned the dishes, and placed them in the dishwasher. This was the guy for me!

Then we married.

After the honeymoon, I returned to work, too, and came in those first two weeks tired, but happy, and cooked the meals while he helped and when we finished dinner, he brought all the dishes to the kitchen and put them in the sink. Two weeks later, he stayed in the kitchen talking to me while I cooked the dinner and afterward, he placed all the dirty dishes on the counter. Then after another two weeks, he read the paper in the living room while I cooked our meal and when he was done, left his dirty dishes on the table. I was livid!

I dissected this and realized that I was no June Cleaver. I was tired, too, and if he thought I was just going to cater to him, he had another think coming. Was this behavior going to continue?

I was so upset after six weeks, I thought about divorce. We were so different. It wasn't going to work.
When we married, I worked as a men's clothing manufacturer representative which had a showroom at the Atlanta Apparel Mart. Working there was good and bad. Good because I wore the sample size of the designer fashions. Bad because I spent a lot of my money on the sample size designer fashions. Good because they sold the sample size designer fashions to me at cost. I had a closet full of gorgeous clothes. One day after hard work at the Mart, I came home in my adorable pastel pink box style top by Diane Von Furstenberg paired with a mid-calf Valentino gray pencil skirt that I bought once while on a break at work. Influenced by Princess Diana, I wore off-white colored pantyhose with black flats and my pearl necklace. I carefully hung up my clothes in the closet and dreaded my next job: making dinner. I grabbed an old t-shirt and shorts to wear while thinking about spaghetti.

I was tired and the tears started to flow. Who understood this dilemma of early married sacrifices? I called a former teacher from high school, who everyone loved and sought advice from because her wisdom was spot on. She was about 8 years older than me. Everyone looked up to her and heeded what was said because she was kind, never judgmental, and gave great advice.

She listened. Then she told me an anecdote of her own to help my suffering. Once she was in a similar position. She was in another state, hours from her parents. She was crying to them on the phone because she now had a 2-year old, her husband traveled for work Monday through Friday and was never home, and she didn't know anyone in her new town. Her only company was her 2-year old.

Her mother inserted, "Honey! Now listen. Your hubby comes home tomorrow from his trip. He'll be tired. You pull yourself together and get in there and make him his favorite meal and his favorite dessert. Stop your crying! I haven't got time to talk to you right now. We can't find your father's teeth!"

Priorities.

"I've Got the Wedding Bell Blues?"

1983 Wedding Dress

Once Upon a Time...

No one said a thing. She asked over and over, "What time is it now?" The answer was always, "Just a few minutes since you last asked."

It was her wedding day. She dressed with her five bridesmaids in the Brides Room of a small Presbyterian Church. She was almost thirty years old and dreamed of this day for a long time. The groom was also thirty. It was their first marriage.

The reception was held in the bride's family front yard in May. The flowering bushes and potted plants were identical in color to the bridesmaids' dresses: Rubrum lily magenta. Their dresses were American Beauty taffeta with a fitting bodice and portrait neckline that had cap sleeves and a longer back hemline. They carried Rubrum lily bouquets in the same color to match their dresses. She wore a candlelight white dress of ivory satin and French re-embroidered lace. The bodice of the gown of pearled Alencon lace featured a deeply scooped neckline and tiny puffed sleeves. The skirt fell from a natural waistline, sweeping back into a chapel length train. A deep border of Alencon lace edged the gown and train.

The bride's headpiece had a wreath of satin roses and forget-me-nots to which the chapel length veil of illusion tulle was attached. Streamers of satin ribbons trailed from the back of the wreath. She carried an all white bouquet of gardenias (her favorite flower), tube roses, and stephanotis with cascading ribbons. Both headpiece and gown were purchased at Regenstein's in Atlanta and were securely packed after the wedding in a box for safekeeping. Still in her closet, it hasn't seen the light of day for 32 years.

The groom and his ushers wore grey tuxes with tails.

And here it was, this beautiful day and the ceremony hadn't started. What time WAS it?

The action was happening upstairs, outside, on the expressway, any-where but in the Bride's room, except for a few hushed whispers. The bride noticed her bridesmaids left the room a lot. Rumor had it that the groom had vanished and her mother was on his tail. Was he going to be a run-away groom?

The congregation was getting antsy because that's all they knew, too. The groom, driving his future-mother-in-law's car with her in the front seat with him, were like bats out of hell heading out of town.

What just happened? The minister asked the groom for the mar-riage license. He did not have it. It was in the glove compartment of his car, which was parked and hidden at the bride's home where the reception was to take place. The car was hidden so that nothing terrible could be done to it.

When the bride's cousin got married, someone wrote in shoe polish on her new husband's car, "Her day. His night." So, this wedding-day-groom was trying to avoid anything like that happening to his foreign-made car.

Luckily, one of the guests was the Chief of Police for the town. He got on his dispatch and notified all the city police officers and the county deputies to allow the bride's mother's car (that same ole Delta 88 lime green Oldsmobile those blondes took on that Hilton Head Beach trip) to pass through without being stopped for speeding. There was even a small police escort with blaring lights from the church to the home of the bride where the marriage license was waiting. That may be an urban legend at this point.

The congregation and bridesmaids did not know the whole story and just thought something was amiss, so that when the groom finally walked into the sanctuary with his best man about thirty minutes late, the crowd laughed and clapped.

The prince hadn't abandoned his princess. And thirty-two years later...still a happily ever after.

The End.

Closet:

Cunning Linguist

To The One I Love

1944 Love Letter

By the time I was in 8th grade, a new high school was built. There was a new football field, school, and parking lot, but we still had to go over to the old campus for our high school basketball games. The 8th graders were situated at the new school in a separate wing, which although we were divided, we still went to pep rallies and student council assemblies for speeches. We felt older and our pictures were even in the high school yearbook. But we were babies by comparison.

I tried to appear more high schoolish by wearing what I saw in the halls when I did get a glimpse of an upper classman. One of my favorites was a solid camel brown ribbed sweater with sleeves to the elbow and a mock turtle neck. I had a plaid black and camel brown A-line skirt. By this time, knee socks were the rage and I wore off-white ones with my new shoes...the 60's saddle shoes by Bass. We called them clodhoppers at my school. They were laced-up black and white and were easily scuffed. You had to use a good bit of white or black shoe polish to clean them. They were something I treasured. My hair was shaped into a bob that curled under right below my chin and my cut bangs popped up at the temples because of my parallel cowlicks. I didn't care, because the rage was turn-under chin length bobs and bangs.

I remembered an English class where we practiced letter writing. We learned all the different parts of the letter: the heading, the body, the salutation, etc. I practiced one at home at the kitchen table (where I did most of my homework) for an assignment due the next day.

Mother watched me and came over to observe my work. She sat down next to me and asked, "May I tell you a story about your father and me? It was when we were writing letters to each other during the war."

I nodded in the affirmative.

She began, "I worried sick about him while he was gone on his Navy missions. You know he was on a destroyer on the outskirts of Italy."

I nodded in the affirmative again (but I didn't remember any of that).

"We exchanged letters as much as possible. However, because it was such a tempestuous time, your father couldn't relay information about his naval activities or his locations. It was very scary. The war office would make sure the letters sent from the young men did not carry any information in them to be intercepted and used against us in the war. There was a saying at that time and it was, 'Loose lips sink ships.' "

I listened. It sounded like a mystery to me. I loved mysteries.

"One time", she continued, "I received a letter from your father that started with a 'Dear Darling', the entire middle part of the letter was totally cut out, then it was signed, 'Love, Your Husband' at the bottom. I thought to myself, 'What did he say? Did he write secrets that should not have been revealed? Will he get in trouble?' "

My eyes widened.

"Of course, I wrote back to my Dear Darling but worried the entire time, weeks on end, until I heard from him again. His answer about the previous cut-out letter was that he didn't have much time to write, wanted just to let me know he was alive, and just cut out the middle all by himself because he was lazy or too tired to write any more than that because he owed me a letter."

Mother kept that letter with her others from daddy. I never saw all those lovely romantic letters until after both my parents passed and I became the keeper of her memories.

Mack Attack

1971 High School Yearbook

I went to elementary, middle, and high school with Mack Neal. He lived next door to my CHILDHOOD-FRIEND. There were lots of kids on that street. I stayed over at CF's house every other weekend to spend the night. The other weekends, she spent the night at mine. We were pretty inseparable. It was more fun at her house because she had an older sister who had friends over at the same time. CHILDHOOD-FRIEND lived on a street where there were lots of children who played outside under the street lights until we were called to come in. As an only child, all these kids at once was fun.

One day in middle school (or really it was called Junior High in the 1960's) when our teacher was absent, we had a male substitute teacher. We were well behaved and not disrespectful. But a substitute teacher was a substitute teacher and it was confusing if you weren't subbing in the same classroom a lot.

The sub was taking roll. He came to Mack's name and called it.

Mack answered, "Present."

The man said, "And what is your first name?"

Mack answered, "Mack."

The substitute responded, "What is your first name?"

"My name is Mack Neal."

"No, son, I have your last name, what is your first name?" the man asked.

And so it went on for a while longer until the old man got it straight.

Mack and I attended school together for 12 years, played as children, were in high school clubs together, and were just forever entwined in our small town.

When he signed my favorite and precious school yearbook for the last time, I thought he would be writing something so profound about all our years together. I thought he would bring up memories I forgot. I thought he respected me so that he would challenge me to make something of myself in the future. I looked forward to seeing those sentimental and heartfelt words written in our last annual.

While reading it, I saw all the effort and thought he put into those last words when he wrote, "It's been real. Mack."

The Inquest

1997 Lunch Bag

One year in the late 1990's, while teaching middle school, we hired a new chorus teacher.

I had a problem.

As an undergraduate, I was a Journalism major with a minor in public relations. After switching to Art from music, I changed majors and I landed in Journalism. I worked for my hometown newspaper in high school and again during the summers when home from college.

The first rule in journalism was to get all the information one could in the first paragraph because you never knew where the editors might cut off your story. If you had all the facts in first, WHO? WHAT? WHEN? WHERE? WHY? HOW? even if the story was longer, the reader might be interested enough to stay with it and continue reading. You wrote the facts first and elaborated in future paragraphs.

My problem was when I usually met someone for the first time, I spewed questions. I would cut to the chase to find out about someone sooner rather than later. Why would you want to wait? What if you found a common denominator from which a friendship might start?

And I was curiously interested in people. Sometimes when I gathered information, I helped solve problems for people. I brought people together when one had what another one needed. I think that was called being "A Connector."

Our new Chorus teacher, with his cafeteria lunch tray, sat down next to me at the teachers' table. I carried my lunch to school in my Fit and Fresh Downtown insulated lunch bag almost every day. It was made of cotton and designed with yellow paisley flowers and had two short brown straps. The wire frame allowed my lunch containers and water bottle to fit in easily. It had a zipper closure and exterior front pocket which is where I kept my napkins and utensils. The extra thick PEVA lining and ice pack kept my meals cool and fresh (like my mother's delicious homemade chicken salad and deviled eggs). I kept it in my kitchen pantry.

When he sat down, I started talking and not thinking a thing about my line of conversation. I proceeded firing a salvo of questions when after about five minutes of inquiry, he picked up his unfinished lunch tray and moved eight seats away to the end of the table to get away from me.

I'm sorry. Was it something I said?

Chatty Cathy

1959 School Picture

My first grade teacher was older than dirt. She may not have been, but her fashion seemed to suggest it: her hair, her eyeglasses, and especially her shoes, which looked orthopedic.

I was constantly moved from desk to desk because I was always getting in trouble for talking. I warmed every seat in my first grade class. I never felt ashamed, really. I remembered still loving elementary school and getting dressed in the morning for school. One of my favorites was a one piece drop waist dress which was black and white checkered from the hips to the knees. The short-sleeved top was solid black with a broad collar with red piping. The outside piping came to a point in front where there was a red bow. Inside the "V" of the neckline was more black and white checkered material. I wore white socks and black ballerina flats. I had on that dress the day we took classroom pictures, although the pictures were not in color. I kept that 1st grade composite picture. I posted that class picture on Facebook. We have all changed, but there were still some faces I recognized.

When I moved back to my hometown as a married adult with children, our SPARE son was a little too chatty. I vented my frustration to a former teacher friend of mine who I knew would understand my problem. She was unique in that way.

This teacher, a now retired Home Economics/Consumer Science teacher, was mentioned in a May 21, 1999 New York Times article as being one of the most reassuring teachers after a copy-cat Columbine shooting at her school. "After hearing the shots, a special-skills teacher at the school, found her daughter, a freshman, and hid with seven other students and a teacher in a closet. The other teacher (my former teacher) recited the 23d Psalm and assured the students they were going to be safe." And they were.

She was not only an inspiration at her school, where she won Teacher of the Year several times, but also was a charismatic public speaker at state Methodist Church conferences. My mother accused me of telling everything I knew and talking too much. But I responded back, "You know who else talks a lot and tells her stories that always make people feel better? That is who I want to be like!"

To make me feel better about my child's situation, she told me her story when she was a little girl growing up. She was a real chatter box and got in trouble because of it. This was frowned upon by her teacher and her principal.

Her family lived in the country at the north end of the county and she attended the only elementary school in the county, which was in-town. One day in first grade, she chatted away, when her teacher, exasperated, didn't know how to keep her quiet and sent her to the principal's office. The principal thought maybe she should go home for the remainder of the day. This was not an uncommon idea in the 1950's.

The principal wanted to call her home. But her parents did not own a phone. The principal called their neighbor's phone. This neighbor walked next door to inform the girl's mother that the principal called and that she needed to come pick up her daughter. Now another dilemma. The child's mother also did not have a car. How was she supposed to retrieve her daughter?

Thanks to this good neighbor, the mother borrowed her neighbor's automobile and drove (a good 15 miles) to the school, picked up her daughter, and brought her home. During the ride home, my teacher friend said she wondered what her mother might say to her and what kind of trouble she might be in. She waited a long time. And eventually, her mother said, "Honey, all this talking is going to make you an interesting adult."

Check back on that New York Times article.

Glossary – Cast of Characters
~in order of appearance~

1. THE HEIR – Like the British press, I gave my children these names for my children. Should be obvious. Named the first-born son this who is OUR PRIDE…

2. THE SPARE – the second-born son AND OUR JOY.

3. THE HOST – a pompous, controlling, sexist, son-of-a-bitch who was totally smart and knew it.

4. Hugh Lee (Hu Le) - ***HUBBY*** (kiss, kiss)

5. MY-ALMOST-BIG-SISTER – as an only child, this childhood neighbor took the place of not having a big sister. Knew me better than anyone and accepted my outrageous behavior (I think.) She was the best memory-keeper that I had of my past. Three years older than me. Remembered my coming home from the hospital as an infant. Our parents were neighbors for 50 years. The ONLY person my mother allowed to let me double date with at an early age because she trusted MY-ALMOST-BIG-SISTER to look after me. Mistake! Matron-of-Honor in my wedding.

6. PARTNER-IN-CRIME – Atlanta born and bred, my tour guide into the world of being a 22-year-old singleton in Buckhead, Atlanta, Georgia. Thank you, soooooooo much! I know to keep many of our stories IN THE VAULT. Bridesmaid in my wedding.

7. FUTURE-VALEDICTORIAN – childhood friend from church and school. Before becoming a doctor and making the big bucks, my parents wanted to pair us together as a couple while we were still in elementary school because he was also an only child and was going to inherit $$. His rich uncle asked his parents to change their baby's name to his own and if they did, he would leave his money to this male child. They did.

8. TIE-ONE-ONA- all I can say about this neighbor…giggle, giggle, giggle. We topped each other's situational humor – not to outdo the other one - but just kept the laughs flowing. We should be joke writers for some TV show. I knew she'd like to be one for ELLEN

or CHELSEA. Still waiting to be told when she is scheduled to compete on FAMILY FEUD.

9. CO-TEACHER - now retired, she was a certified elementary school teacher and I was a certified high school teacher. We met in the middle – middle school, that is. She brought the sweetness to the classroom and I brought the zany. We worked TOGETHER in the SAME CLASSROOM (2 women sharing a workspace – think about it) for 10 years. A good ying/yang fit. Very close friends.

10. PE-TEACHER – FSU fanatic and told the SLUTS (Southern Ladies Under Tremendous Stress) just the right dirty-joke or story we needed to hear. (Don't let her mother know.)

11. THE-GIRL-I-LOOKED-UP-TO- this is the 2-year-older-gal who I did almost everything with in high school – cheerleading, girls' trio, double-dating, you name it. I kept HER out of trouble (don't ask). Our hubbies were besties and we have traveled together as couples around the globe.

12. NANNOOO – oh, my. Will never be forgotten. Was our third partner during our almost decade-long-Atlanta antics. We three were called "The Three Amigos" or "The Three Stooges" because the three of us were blonde and people (especially inebriated ones) confused us with each other. RIP, NANNOOO.

13. CHILDHOOD FRIEND – from kindergarten thru high school, almost every Friday night we spent the night together. I don't think there was anything we didn't share, especially one particular boy-friend who screwed us both over.

Thanks, kudos, and 5-stars go to Greg Marshall, Scarlett Gibson, Susan Beaumont, Jane Heaberlin, Carolyn McDevitt, Bonnie Marshall (no relation to Greg), Donna Moore, and Deborah Lincoln. I don't see how they stood it. They put up with me during the best of times and the worst of times. A special recognition goes to Mr. Tom Hay, past owner and publisher of the "Rockdale Citizen" newspaper, who told me when I was a teenager that I should be a writer. I wish I could say, "How do you like me now?" Love goes out to my family: my mother who bestowed on me the joy and dramatics of storytelling, my father who gave me his humor DNA, my children who inspired (were patsies for) many of the stories, and my hubby who puts up with my antics because he said he wished for a wife that could challenge him.

Be careful what you wish for.

Hey! I've got more wicked stories to expose.

COMING SOON:
SHE'S A KEEPER ~ anecdotes from a Southern Girl's Attic.

My SHE'S A KEEPER ~ bombshells from a Southern Girl's Basement is in the works.

Stay tuned! And thanks for reading!

- Lee St.John

Like Lee on her Facebook page at:
https://www.facebook.com/leestjohnauthor

Visit her website at:
http://www.leestjohnauthor.com/

ABOUT THE AUTHOR

When Lee St. John was a little girl, her mother would say, "If you don't behave, I'm going put you in a paper sack and throw you away!"

But she couldn't help herself. Lee St. John does not have a "pause" button! In fact, she never hesitates to express and do what most people only wish they had the nerve to say and do. As a born and bred Southern only child whose behavior horrified her parents, she is used to getting what she wants...and what she wants most right now is for her sons to pay attention to her! Finding keepsakes in her closets trigger memories of her life, her family, her students, her friends and she wants to share with them, but they are not giving her the time of day.

So, she wrote them down. NOW she has their attention.

Made in the USA
Charleston, SC
15 November 2015